T0295698

Islamic Capital Markets

This book offers a unique, in-depth, and up-to-date overview of Islamic banking and finance, capital markets, and sukuks at the grassroots level. It deals with one of the most potent and increasingly popular financial instruments. It defines and explores the differences between conventional and Sukuk bonds and also examines the integration of Sukuk in various country contexts and both Muslim and non-Muslim economies.

The book consists of five core topics. First, it describes the evolution of the Islamic finance industry and capital markets; second, it discusses the basic features and instruments of Islamic banking; and third, it illustrates the current state of capital markets and Islamic finance. The book then examines the development of Sukuk in Islamic capital markets and Shariah perspectives and, finally, briefly discusses the structure of Sukuks and its development in the context of Pakistan.

In a nutshell, this book provides a basic understanding of Islamic financial instruments, their implementation in different regions, and their points of differentiation from conventional modes of finance; therefore, it will be a useful addition to the literature for scholars, researchers, and students of Islamic banking and finance.

Imam Uddin, Ph.D., is an associate professor in the Department of Accounting and Finance at the Institute of Business Management (IoBM), Karachi, Pakistan.

Rabia Sabri is a senior lecturer and HoD at the Institute of Business Management (IoBM), Karachi, Pakistan.

M. Ishaq Bhatti is a professor of finance and financial econometrics and the founding director of the Islamic Banking and Finance Programme at La Trobe University, Australia.

Muhammad Omer Rafique is an Islamic finance Shariah scholar with half a decade of experience in teaching and research.

Muhammad AsadUllah is a senior lecturer at College of Economic & Social Development (CESD), Institute of Business Management (IoBM), Karachi, Pakistan.

Islamic Business and Finance Series
Series Editor: Ishaq Bhatti

There is an increasing need for western politicians, financiers, bankers, and indeed the western business community in general to have access to high quality and authoritative texts on Islamic financial and business practices. Drawing on expertise from across the Islamic world, this new series will provide carefully chosen and focused monographs and collections, each authored/edited by an expert in their respective field all over the world.

The series will be pitched at a level to appeal to middle and senior management in both the western and the Islamic business communities. For the manager with a western background the series will provide detailed and up-to-date briefings on important topics; for the academics, postgraduates, business communities, manager with western and an Islamic background the series will provide a guide to best practice in business in Islamic communities around the world, including Muslim minorities in the west and majorities in the rest of the world.

Islamic Monetary Economics
Finance and Banking in Contemporary Muslim Economies
Edited by Taha Eğri and Zeyneb Hafsa Orhan

Islamic Capital Markets
The Structure, Formation and Management of Sukuk
Imam Uddin, Rabia Sabri, M. Ishaq Bhatti, Muhammad Omer Rafique and Muhammad AsadUllah

Institutional Islamic Economics and Finance
Edited by Ahsan Shafiq

For more information about this series, please visit: www.routledge.com/ Islamic-Business-and-Finance-Series/book-series/ISLAMICFINANCE

Islamic Capital Markets

The Structure, Formation and
Management of Sukuk

**Imam Uddin, Rabia Sabri, M. Ishaq
Bhatti, Muhammad Omer Rafique and
Muhammad AsadUllah**

Routledge
Taylor & Francis Group

LONDON AND NEW YORK

First published 2022
by Routledge
4 Park Square, Milton Park, Abingdon, Oxon OX14 4RN

and by Routledge
605 Third Avenue, New York, NY 10158

Routledge is an imprint of the Taylor & Francis Group, an informa business

© 2022 Imam Uddin, Rabia Sabri, M. Ishaq Bhatti, Muhammad Omer Rafique and Muhammad AsadUllah

The right of Imam Uddin, Rabia Sabri, M. Ishaq Bhatti, Muhammad Omer Rafique and Muhammad AsadUllah to be identified as authors of this work has been asserted in accordance with sections 77 and 78 of the Copyright, Designs and Patents Act 1988.

British Library Cataloguing-in-Publication Data
A catalogue record for this book is available from the British Library

Library of Congress Cataloging-in-Publication Data
Names: Uddin, Imam, author. | Sabri, Rabia, author. | Bhatti, M. Ishaq, author. | Rafique, Muhammad Omer, author. | AsadUllah, Muhammad (Senior lecturer at CESD), author.
Title: Islamic capital markets : the structure, formation and management of sukuk / Imam Uddin, Rabia Sabri, M. Ishaq Bhatti, Muhammad Omer Rafique and Muhammad AsadUllah.
Description: Milton Park, Abingdon, Oxon ; New York, NY : Routledge, 2022. | Series: Islamic business and finance | Includes bibliographical references and index.
Identifiers: LCCN 2021047767 (print) | LCCN 2021047768 (ebook) | ISBN 9781032153506 (hardback) | ISBN 9781032153520 (paperback) | ISBN 9781003243755 (ebook)
Subjects: LCSH: Banks and banking—Religious aspects—Islam. | Bonds (Islamic law) | Bonds—Religious aspects—Islam. | Bonds—Islamic countries. | Capital market—Islamic countries. | Capital market (Islamic law)
Classification: LCC HG5818.A3 U33 2022 (print) | LCC HG5818.A3 (ebook) | DDC 332.63/2091767—dc23
LC record available at https://lccn.loc.gov/2021047767
LC ebook record available at https://lccn.loc.gov/2021047768

ISBN: 978-1-032-15350-6 (hbk)
ISBN: 978-1-032-15352-0 (pbk)
ISBN: 978-1-003-24375-5 (ebk)

DOI: 10.4324/9781003243755

Typeset in Times New Roman
by Apex CoVantage, LLC

Contents

Figures

Authors' Biography

Dr. Ishaq Bhatti

ORCID: http://orcid.org/0000-0002-5027-7871

Dr. Ishaq Bhatti, Professor, La Trobe University, Australia. Dr. Bhatti is a renowned educationist in Australia having the honor of developing Australia's first ever Islamic Banking & Finance program and is currently serving as the Director Masters in Islamic Banking & Finance course at La Trobe University. He is an author of more than 70 articles, 3 books and a member of the editorial board of various economics/statistics journal.

Dr. Imam Uddin

ORCID: https://orcid.org/0000-0003-2374-7003

Dr. Imam Uddin holds a Ph.D. in Islamic Business and Finance from the University of Karachi, emphasizing rules and regulations of Islamic Banking and Finance in the Pakistani context. Additionally, he furthered his Islamic Banking and Finance knowledge by attending numerous courses: Specialization in Islamic Jurisprudence, LLB, and PGD in Islamic Banking and Finance. His areas of expertise include Islamic Banking and Finance, Islamic Economics, Islamic Jurisprudence, Fiscal Laws and Humanities. He has got more than 15 years of experience in teaching, research, product development, product management, and Shariah compliance. He has authored various book chapters and research papers on Islamic Economics and Finance. Currently, he is serving as Associate Professor in the Department of Accounting and Finance at the Institute of Business Management (IoBM), Karachi. Previously, he worked with DHA Suffa University Karachi, Mohammad Ali Jinnah University Karachi, and University of Balochistan Quetta & Center for Islamic Economics (CIE). He has also served the Islamic Banking Group (AIBG) of the National Bank of Pakistan (NBP) as Vice President in the Compliance Group and Product Development Wing.

He tries to develop intellectuals for the Islamic banking industry by delivering lectures, conducting workshops, and organizing seminars at the national and international levels.

Rabia Sabri

ORCID ID 0000-0002-9135-2137

Rabia Sabri is a qualified Chartered Management Accountant (FCMA) and MBA in Accounting and Finance. Currently, she is pursuing MS Finance from Bahria University and Chartered Financial Analyst level (CFA) from CFAI. She is working as Senior Lecturer and HoD with IoBM. She has more than 15 years of teaching and corporate experience. She has taught Accounting, Finance, Corporate Reporting Economics courses in various universities in Karachi and served in two universities of Saudi Arabia and also taught ACCA and PIPFA courses. Her area of research is financial reporting and analysis of equity and fixed income securities.

Muhammad Omer Rafique

ORCID: https://orcid.org/0000-0001-9051-0044

Muhammad Omer Rafique is an Islamic finance Shariah scholar with half a decade of experience in teaching and research. He is currently pursuing his Ph.D. from the University of Malaya Kuala Lumpur in Islamic finance. He has issued more than 3000 verdicts on several Shariah issues. He has Shariah audited many commercial organizations and helped them comply with Shariah standards.

Muhammad AsadUllah

ORCID: https://orcid.org/0000-0002-6690-5457

Muhammad AsadUllah holds an M.Phil. in Business Management from IoBM to be followed by a Ph.D. in Finance. Initially, he joined EMEC-IoBM as a facilitator for training projects. He is currently working as a senior lecturer at CESD, IoBM. He has also worked as a visiting faculty in various business schools. His research interest includes Panel Data Analysis of secondary data from different sectors. He has presented various papers in national and international conferences. He has published 27 research papers and presented ten conference papers in national and international conferences.

Foreword

Sukuk have become indispensable instruments without which the Islamic finance industry would not have developed in the manner it has over the last half century. This handbook provides a concise guide to the many types of Sukuk available, the wide range being made possible by the rich offering of Islamic financial contracts. The attraction of Sukuk for institutional and private investors is that they are liquid assets which can be purchased and sold in a secondary market, fulfilling a similar function to bonds, but being acceptable financial assets from a *Shariah* perspective, whereas Riba-based bonds are unacceptable.

Without Sukuk the Takaful Islamic insurance industry would not have developed, as Takaful operators cannot be overweight in shares, especially operators providing medical, vehicle, or property contents insurance. These involve monthly premiums being collected on an annual cycle with investment in liquid instruments of short duration. With family Takaful, which is often marketed as a mortgage protection policy, investing in equities with Sukuk accounting for a much smaller portion of the portfolio makes financial sense.

The other major institutional investors in Sukuk are *Shariah*-compliant managed funds. Although dedicated Sukuk funds only account for a small portion of the market, equity funds, the dominant player in the market, usually have a mandate which permits some Sukuk holding. This is a precautionary measure, as they will want to hold equity when markets are performing well and expectations are favorable, but increase Sukuk holdings as a defensive strategy if there are conditions of uncertainty.

Most Sukuks are corporate, originated by companies that do not want to dilute their shares by further equity issuance. Sovereign Sukuk have increased in importance in recent years, with governments of Muslim majority countries taping the market on a regular basis. Interestingly, Western countries have now started to enter the market, including the government of the United Kingdom. They were less concerned with raising large amounts of funding, the major aim being to establish a benchmark rate of return for sterling-denominated Sukuk to enhance London's reputation as a global Islamic financial center.

Readers of this handbook will be able to appreciate the significance of these wider issues. There is a particular focus on Pakistan, whose experience has lessons for other developing countries with emerging financial markets. There can be no doubt that Sukuk will have an important role to play in the future of Islamic financial intermediation. This concise guide should help ensure that the basic rules of Sukuk issuance are understood and the readership is better informed.

Professor Rodney Wilson
Emeritus Professor, Durham University, United Kingdom

Preface

Islamic finance has brought several revolutions in the world, one of them is the shift from Western terminologies to Islamic terminologies. New words are introduced in the field of finance and economics. The word "Sukuk" is now being used instead of bonds and T-bills. There is a dire need of introducing these concepts with all their legalities and complications to portray the reality of these Shariah instruments. In a Shariah audit in a reputable charitable organization, the interviewee was not able to understand the word "Ijarah," he confined the word Ijrah to the Ijarah lease practiced in the banks, while any service contract is Ijarah.

Islamic finance after success in banking moved toward capital markets, as it is the inevitable part of any economy. The Riba-free, Ijarah capital markets solutions like Sukuk have immense potential, and these way outs can be a great source of Islamizing the whole economy. The proper application of these Sukuk Shariah rulings is pivotal to protect the sanctity of the prefix Islamic and ensure Shariah compliance.

Pakistan is one of the pioneers in Islamic finance in terms of human resources and Shariah expertise. Due to several reasons, the growth of Islamic banking has been steady throughout the last four decades. The Pakistani capital market has immense potential for the growth of Sukuk and Islamic bonds. This industry is still in its infancy stage.

This book is intended to give a comprehensive overview of Sukuk from its concept and history to the legitimacy debate and growing opportunity for Sukuk. Therefore, this book can be a reference book for Sukuk write-ups as well as a textbook for capital market students. All the authors have contributed in almost all chapters, due to which it hardly seems that the book has multiple authors. The references are authentic, and the content is well organized to understand the concept and structures of Islamic bonds.

1 Evolution of Islamic Financial & Capital Market

Rabia Sabri, Imam Uddin, Muhammad Omer Rafique, Muhammad AsadUllah, and M. Ishaq Bhatti

Introduction

Human beings, since antiquity, are involved in expanding their financial resources and statuses by earning profits from different activities. These activities are usually associated with putting appropriate capital values into multiple tangible and intangible resources around the built environment and getting outcomes of financial nature, for which, an increased and superseding capital value is presumably obtained by the participating parties. Within this conventional fabric of business, there are many social and ideological limitations that have been addressed and resolved by developing some entirely new financing models in different parts of the world. In this regard, Islamic banking is relatively a newborn and tremendously prevailing model (Mordor Intelligence, 2019), which resolves the limitations contained within the conventional business and financing fabric, in order to let the global Muslims community (known as *Ummah*) participate and earn benefits from the previously existing financing system, without any ideological constraint or limitation.

Islamic Banking and Financing

The banking and financing vision of Islam is basically associated with the concept of eliminating interests and relevant financial elements from the framework of financing and business in order to prevail a mutually system of profit and loss sharing (Cattelan, 2009). In other words, Islamic banking and financing promises its participating clients and parties a mutually beneficial model which outlines money borrowing, lending, and investment-related functions on a risk-sharing basis (Khan & Bhatti, 2008; Zarqa, 1983). In this manner, when a party invests in some macro- or micro-business activity through a financial institution (such as a bank), it is

DOI: 10.4324/9781003243755-1

duly informed that the invested capital can turn either into a pre-assumed profit or into a loss, depending upon the activities and uncertainties in the surrounding environment and its affecting social and political elements (Mirakhor & Zaidi, 2007). This, according to Khan and Bhatti (2008), gives an opportunity for parties to evaluate and assess the productivity features of capital instead of realizing its value upon conventional interest rates – a framework of evaluating capital in the conventional financing industry. This not only ensures the financing party an optimal rate of capital formulation but also allows it to extract a fair and just profit, earned in accord to the surrounding corporate environmental conditions. A more precise definition of Islamic financing framework is outlined by El-Gamal (2006) is prohibiting the involvement of Riba (interest) of any kind in any business activity. In this respect, whatever nature of business is conducted by the financing party (be it an individual, a corporate group, a financial institution, a money lending organization, etc.), it is always free from the interest that is usually considered a legitimate capital securing value. According to Ahmed (2011), this system seeks to develop such a financing framework in which a financing party acts in accord with the socioeconomic regulations of Islam, thus maintaining the respect and value of the surrounding cultural fabric.

If it is investigated through the course of history, the crude concept of Islamic financing and banking was informally present in the last years of the Caliphate and different non-standardized financing and interest-free money lending or borrowing activities were found to be carried out on a micro-scale in the 8th century's newly Islamized peninsula of Arabia (Labib, 1969; Banaji, 2007). Furthermore, those activities were mainly associated with the concept of eliminating Riba from financing and money lending activities – an association that became the core of Islamic financing and banking tools for the coming ages, when Islam did expand and its concepts were documented and preached in many parts of the world. However, no implementation or standardization was carried out until the early 1900s when the rise of Western conventional banking and its capitalistic approach did start creating problems for the socioeconomic condition of Muslim countries (Khorshid, 2009).

During this era, many money-saving and Riba-free money lending institutions were established, which overall failed to attract Muslim populations to the way of their operations. In the meantime, the ideas of mutual profit–loss sharing in financial activities were presented by multiple researchers such as Qureshi (1946), Mawdūdī (1955), and Ahmad (1952), which seemed more attractive to Islamic financing and retail banking communities around the globe. Moreover, these ideas were further elaborated and generalized by scholars such as Uzair (1955), Siddiqi (1961), and Al Najjar and Swarup (1971), who collectively urged for the implementation of a justified and regularized Islamic financing system in their works. This, along with the socio-political changes in the Middle Eastern and South Asian countries (including Pakistan), made it more necessary for the global Islamic community to start thinking about the implementation of the Islamic financing model in a serious manner (Nagaoka, 2012).

Finally, it happened in the year 1975 that the first Islamic bank with a standardized operating framework (approved by multiple religious bodies and economists) started working by the name of Dubai Islamic Bank in the UAE. In the coming years, almost all Muslim countries and their financial regulating bodies did follow this standardized procedure for Islamic banking and many Islamic banking institutions with prolific portfolios started operating within their boundaries. It has been estimated that today there are more than 500 Islamic banks operating in different Islamic and non-Islamic countries with multiple branches and reputable ways of operations around the globe (The Banker's, 2010), which was doubled by 2018 (Thomson Reuters, 2018). Furthermore, it has been estimated that global assets associated with Shariah-compliant Islamic financing institutions have reached over $2.5 trillion, with the contribution of Islamic banks of Saudi Arabia, Iran, Malaysia, UAE, Egypt, and Pakistan (Thomson Reuters, 2018).

The feasible concept of Islamic banking is now starting to soar in the global financial markets due to its reliable and much-clarified framework of operations, and many conventional banks in different Islamic and non-Islamic countries have developed their own controlled Islamic financing bodies and branches, to attract the general population with a relatively new idea of banking and finance (Bukhari et al., 2013). This can be verified by the results of a 2010 survey conducted by *The Banker*, which revealed that the Islamic financing industry around the globe has enjoyed a compound annual growth rate of 23.46% in the last four years, and their operations remained completely unaffected from the global financial crisis of 2008 (The Banker's, 2010).

Basic Features and Instruments

As the basic and most fundamental concept behind Islamic financing is the elimination of interest from financial transactions, many forms of instruments and their standardized terminologies have been developed by Islamic banks and other regulatory authorities around the globe. According to Khan and Bhatti (2008), these instruments and features are the Islamic version of the same conventional banking and financing operations, practiced in many countries since the last century under the terminology of sale-based and lease-based operations. However, these instruments do not carry with them any Ribah or other related financial elements, which are considered as limitations for Islamic banking and financing. Some of the major features and instruments are succinctly outlined later, the details would require a separate handbook on each of these instruments. However, we would talk in a bit more detail about these features in the upcoming chapter under the heading of structures of Sukuk.

Musharakah

The term *Musharakah* can be understood as a joint venture, which is created between two financing parties in a single investment program. In this venture, the profits obtained on the investment are shared by both parties on the basis of their financing value, and losses are shared mutually by both parties according to the appropriate ratios of their investments (Farhad & Ali, 1994; Kazi, 2020). In this regard, the financing parties may include an independent client venturing with a financial institution, two financial institutions venturing together in a business, etc. (Arshad & Ismail, 2010).

Mudarabah

Mudarabah (or profit-sharing) is also a type of financial venture in which one party allots finances to another party for investing in any commercial enterprise or other corporate activity (Qazi, 2008). In this manner, the party that finances becomes the partner of another party that handles the specialized operations required in the management of these finances. In other words, both parties become partners in single investment activity, with operations and financial management being the domain of the party upon which finances are invested.

Murabahah

This feature of Islamic financing is strikingly similar to the concept of the rent-to-own model of goods and services practiced in many countries. In this type of agreement, any fixed asset is allotted on rent to the client over an agreement of pre-determined rent, and when the term of renting is finished, the client becomes the sole owner of an asset by paying the current value of it. In this manner, the financing party earns a pre-determined profit over the good rented to the client (Al-Ameen, 2000).

Ijarah

Under the procedure of Ijarah, the financing party "leases" any product to the client with an agreement bounded by a particular period of time and amount of money. In this process, no interest is taken from the client, and if at any time, the client wants to own the product legally, he or she can simply do it by paying the remaining value (actual value minus leased money) of the product (Ameer & Ansari, 2014).

Salam

In Islamic financing terminology, *Salam* is an agreement that is made between two parties on the basis of selling a product but receiving its payment in a later period of time. However, in this agreement, the product should be anything other than currencies, precious metals, and products or currencies made of these precious metals (Muneeza et al., 2011).

Takaful

Takaful is one of the most common financing procedures practiced in the Islamic financing industry. Under this procedure, a client protects his/her investments from loss by combining investment with multiple people and thus saving his capital from any uncertainty or misfortune. The return on this investment is also based on the collective loss or collective profit, which have different impacts in the cases of individual and collective investments (Swartz & Coetzer, 2010).

Sukuk

The idea of Sukuk in financing terminology is referred to as Islamic bonds. These are financial certificates that are issued against a pre-determined amount of money and are free of conventional interest-based activities in their structure and reselling (Godlewski et al., 2013). This instrument is to be discussed in detail, in the later sections of this study.

Islamic Finance in Capital Markets

Capital markets are an integral part of any economy. It injects the life blood that is financing to the financial system of any country (Marshall & Stiglitz, 1992). Capital markets are a vital part of a capitalist economy that works because they transfer money from the individuals that have it to those that need it for effective use (Black & Gilson, 1998).

For the selling of financial instruments such as equity and debt instruments, capital markets are used. Equities are securities that are shares of ownership in a corporation. Debt securities are interest-bearing IOUs, such as shares. These markets are classified into two distinct subgroups: primary markets, where investors sell new equity stock and bond issues, and secondary markets that trade current securities.

Individual investors who purchase securities directly from the issuing company are connected to the primary markets. Main offerings or initial public offerings (IPOs) are considered to be these securities. It sells its bonds and stocks to large-scale and financial institutions, such as hedge funds and mutual funds, when a company goes public. On the other side, the secondary market comprises platforms regulated by a regulatory agency, such as the Securities and Exchange Commission (SEC), where traders trade in real or already released securities (Kakarot-Handtke, 2012). In the secondary sector, issuing companies do not have a portion. An example of a secondary market is the Pakistan Stock Exchange (PSX).

The financial system cannot be Islamized without rectifying the haram element from the capital markets (Hassan & Mahlknecht, 2011; Salman, 2005). Mostly found haram elements are impermissible speculation, future trading, interest-based investments, short selling, etc. (Lahsasna & Lin, 2012). These activities contradict the golden rules of the Islamic economy.

Slowly, the Islamic financial market has grown to accept activities relating to capital markets (Thomas, 2007). The rectification process is a marathon. McMillen (2006) stated that we are witnessing the first phases of the long-articulated exhortation to establish capital markets for shares and acquisitions that conform with the values and precepts of Islamic Shariah, including secondary markets.

Sukuk has been a great revolution in the capital markets. It has changed the game of investment in many countries. Instead of interest-based bonds, derivatives, and treasury bills, people especially Muslims tend to invest in Sukuk. Ahmed et al. (2020) defined Sukuk as "Sukuk refers to securities characterized as compliant with Islamic Shariah rules and with the principles of investment which prohibit and prevent dealings with interest charges."

Islamic Capital Markets Today

In 2019, the Islamic capital market sector reports enhanced improvements. The sector accounts for 26.5% of IFSI assets globally and is worth approximately USD 645.7 billion. In 2019, similar to 2018, Sukūk (Islamic Bonds) recorded double-digit growth of 22.2% and still clearly dominates the Islamic capital markets in terms of asset share. The solid performance was primarily attributed to strong sovereign and plurilateral issuances to fund in key Islamic finance markets, as well as to a rise in corporate issuances in some territories in 2019. Islamic funds bounced back strongly in 2019, in comparison to the pattern seen in the global stock markets in 2018, posting the dual-digit rise of 29.8% in terms of assets under management (AuM) and a 3.8% rise in the number of Islamic funds compared to 2018 (Islamic Financial Services Board, 2020).

References

Ahmad, S. M. (1952). *Economics of Islam*. Adam Publishers.

Ahmed, E. R., Islam, A., & Hashim, F. (2020). *Sukuk history and development*. University of Nizaw. https://doi.org/10.4018/978-1-7998-0218-1.ch036

Ahmed, H. (2011). Defining ethics in Islamic finance: Looking beyond legality. *Eighth International Conference on Islamic Economics & Finance: Sustainable Growth and Inclusive Economic Development from an Islamic Perspective*, 19–21.

Al-Ameen, H. (2000). *Al-Mudarabah Al-Shareyah Wa Tatbiqatuha Alhaditha*, 1–66. https://esytrunojoyo.files.wordpress.com/2016/01/al-mudharabah-syariyah.pdf

Al Najjar, M. A., & Swarup, R. (1971). *Marketing of dates in Iraq*. Agric Mark Nagpur.

Ameer, M. H., & Ansari, M. S. (2014). Islamic banking: Ijarah and conventional leasing. *Developing Country Studies*, *4*(9), 126–129.

Arshad, N. C., & Ismail, A. G. (2010). Shariah parameters for Musharakah contract: A comment. *International Journal of Business and Social Science*, *1*(1).

Banaji, J. (2007). Islam, the Mediterranean and the rise of capitalism. *Historical Materialism*, *15*(1), 47–74.

The Banker's. (2010). *Top 500 Islamic financial institutions*. https://www.thebanker.com/Reports/Special-Reports/Top-500-Islamic-financial-institutions

Black, B. S., & Gilson, R. J. (1998). Venture capital and the structure of capital markets: Banks versus stock markets. *Journal of Financial Economics*, *47*(3), 243–277.

Bukhari, K. S., Awan, H. M., & Ahmed, F. (2013). An evaluation of corporate governance practices of Islamic banks versus Islamic bank windows of conventional banks: A case of Pakistan. *Management Research Review*, *36*(4), 400–416.

Cattelan, V. (2009). From the concept of haqq to the prohibitions of riba, gharar and maysir in Islamic finance. *International Journal of Monetary Economics and Finance*, *2*(3–4), 384–397.

El-Gamal, M. A. (2006). *Islamic finance: Law, economics, and practice*. Cambridge University Press.

Farhad, N., & Ali, R. (1994). *Islamic economic systems*. Academic Press.

Godlewski, C. J., Turk-Ariss, R., & Weill, L. (2013). Sukuk vs. conventional bonds: A stock market perspective. *Journal of Comparative Economics*, *41*(3), 745–761.

Hassan, K., & Mahlknecht, M. (2011). *Islamic capital markets: Products and strategies* (Vol. 609). John Wiley & Sons.

Irfan, Qazi, Murabaha Financing vs. Lending on Interest (July 22, 2008). Available at SSRN: https://ssrn.com/abstract=1803651 or http://dx.doi.org/10.2139/ssrn.1803651

Islamic Financial Services Board. (2020). *Stability report 2020*. Islamic Financial Services Board.

Kakarot-Handtke, E. (2012). *Primary and secondary markets*. Levy Economics Institute of Bard College Working Paper 741. Levy Economics Institute.

Kazi, R. R. (2020). Dual legal framework in Islamic capital markets: Issues and problems. In *Handbook of research on theory and practice of global Islamic finance* (pp. 524–546). IGI Global.

Khan, M. M., & Bhatti, M. I. (2008). Development in Islamic banking: A financial risk-allocation approach. *The Journal of Risk Finance, 9*(1).

Khorshid, A. (2009). *Understanding derivatives within Islamic finance* (Khorshid, A., Ed.). Euromoney Encyclopedia of Islamic Finance.

Labib, S. Y. (1969). Capitalism in medieval Islam. *Journal of Economic History,* 79–96.

Lahsasna, A., & Lin, L. S. (2012). Issues in Islamic capital markets: Islamic bond/ sukuk. *3rd International Conference on Business and Economic Research (3rd ICBER 2012) Proceeding,* 495–512.

Marshall, A., & Stiglitz, J. E. (1992). Capital markets and economic fluctuations in capitalist economies. *European Economic Review North-Holland, 36,* 269–306.

Mawdūdī, A. A. (1955). *The economic problem of man and its Islamic solution.* Markazi Maktaba Jama'at-eislami Pakistan.

McMillen, M. J. T. (2006). Islamic capital markets: Developments and issues. *Capital Markets Law Journal, 1*(2), 136–172. https://doi.org/10.1093/cmlj/kml015

Mirakhor, A., & Zaidi, I. (2007). Profit-and-loss sharing contracts in Islamic finance. *Handbook of Islamic Banking, 49,* 25–37.

Mordor Intelligence. (2019). *Global Islamic finance market – growth, trends, and forecast (2018–2024).* Mordor Intelligence.

Muneeza, A., Yusuf, N. N. A. N., & Hassan, R. (2011). The possibility of application of salam in Malaysian Islamic banking system. *Humanomics, 27.*

Nagaoka, S. (2012). Critical overview of the history of Islamic economics: Formation, transformation, and new horizons. *Asian and African Area Studies, 11*(2), 114–136.

Qureshi, A. I. (1946). *Islam and the theory of interest.* Islamic Press.

Salman, S. A. (2005). *Islamic capital market products: Developments and challenges.* https://zulkiflihasan.files.wordpress.com/2008/06/icm.pdf

Siddiqi, A. H. (1961). *Islamic state.* International Islamic Publishers.

Swartz, N. P., & Coetzer, P. (2010). Takaful: An Islamic insurance instrument. *Journal of Development and Agricultural Economics, 2*(10), 333–339.

Thomas, A. (2007). Securitization in Islamic finance. In *Islamic finance: The regulatory challenge* (pp. 257–270). Wiley Online Library.

Thomson Reuters. (2018). *Islamic finance development report.* https://ceif.iba.edu. pk/pdf/Reuters-Islamic-finance-development-report2018.pdf

Uzair, M. (1955). *An outline of interestless banking.* Raihan Publications.

Zarqa, M. A. (1983). Stability in an interest-free Islamic economy: A note. *Pakistan Journal of Applied Economics, 2*(2), 181–188.

2   Development of Sukuk in Islamic Capital Markets

Imam Uddin, Rabia Sabri, Muhammad Omer Rafique, Muhammad AsadUllah, and M. Ishaq Bhatti

Introduction

Sukuk (as explained shortly in the previous sections) is one of the financial instruments employed widely throughout the global Islamic financing industry. This instrument not only remains a widely debated element in different capital markets but also promises to bring equivalent benefits as investment certificates to different investing parties. For this reason, before getting into its structure and manner of operations, a close overview of its origin and developments in the Islamic finance industry is necessary to be made part of this study. Furthermore, neutral limelight over its characteristics, composition elements, and placements in Shariah-oriented Islamic capital markets would be an advantageous step for this study to cover, before getting into its operational details.

Sukuk in Islamic Capital Markets

Historical Perspective

The plural of the term sakk means "certificate" or "order of payment," which is the Arabic word Sukuk (Khan & Watson, 2003). Pre-modern Muslim communities used Sukuk as a type of paper reflecting financial commitments arising from commercial and other commercial practices (Jaffer, 2004). In the Middle Ages, a sakk was a written promise to pay for goods when they were shipped and was used to avoid having to carry money over difficult terrain (Vallely, 2006). These Sukuk were exported and distributed around the world across several nations. The idea and the word sakk were conveyed to Europe by Jewish traders from the Islamic world (Braudel, 1995, p. 817). The modern Western word "cheque" seems to have been derived from the Arabic word "sakk" (Salah, 2014).

DOI: 10.4324/9781003243755-2

The origins of Sukuk, which is in nutshell a certificate of beneficial owner-ship rights in a pool of underlying assets which do not represent true owner-ship, but a right to returns for its holders, can be traced back to the early 17th century's Ottoman Empire's system of tax-farming known as *Esham* – selling of equal shares of tax revenues collected from a tax-farm (or privately owned business). In this system, a tax-farm (tax-generating business in a state) was auctioned to a private party with the highest bid of tax collection for a lifetime basis. In this manner, the ownership of stream of revenue for bidder and gov-ernment was securitized with the generated revenue (although uncertain) of tax-farm being divided into equal shares for further selling (Cizakca, 2010). This system of *Esham* was a transformed product of a 14th-century system of tax collection, called the *Malikane* system (Cizakca, 2010). Therefore, if we go back into the pages of history, it is revealed that Muslim countries and their financing industry were formally developed and functioning on its Riba-free framework long before the introduction of interest-based conventional financing system (Berber, 2014).

One more tradition from Islamic history denotes the use of the word Sukuk, although it was not an investment instrument. Under the rule of Khalifah al-Marwan ibn al-Hakam, Sukuk can be traced back to the 1st century AH during the Umayyad Caliphate, as reported by Imam Malik in Al-Muwatta, Book 31, Number 31.19.444:

Yahya told me from Malik that, at the time of Marwan ibn al-Hakam, he had heard that receipts (Sukuk) were given to people for the prod-ucts of the al-Jar market. Before taking delivery of the goods, people bought and sold the receipts (Sukuk) amongst themselves. Zayd bin Thabit and one of Rasulullah's Companions (SAW) went to Marwan and said, "Marwan!" Do you make halal (permissible) usury? He said: "With Allah, I seek shelter! And what's that?" He said, "These (Sukuk) receipts that people buy and sell before they take delivery of the goods." Therefore, Marwan sent a guard to follow them and take them from the hands of people and return to their owners.

(Al Qurtabi, 2008)

Now, considering Sukuk, it runs basically over two distinct elements in the modern Islamic financing system: generation of revenue and securiti-zation of revenue (Mohammed, 2014). As discussed earlier succinctly, the tax-farming system of *Esham* did not contain the first element in its frame-work, but it had with it the concept of securitization of an already exist-ing stream of revenue to a particular party. Therefore, for knowing this first constituent and its origin in modern-day Sukuk, we should consider another 15th-century Ottoman process of cash generation which was then called

Waqf. These *Waqfs,* according to Schoon (2009) and Cizakca (2010), were authorities established with cash capital and had to invest this capital to finance the charity for which they had been established. In its operations, the *Waqfs* invested their capital through a process of sale-lease back-repurchase transaction or *Istaglal* that is buying of a property or asset by a financing institution from an individual, then allotting it to the same individual on rent, and finally transferring the property or asset after a particular amount of time over the current price to the same individual (Schoon, 2009). This type of sale and leaseback purchase process can be clearly seen within the modern Sukuk *Al-ijarah* transactions (Cizakca, 2010), and thus, we find the second main constituent of modern-day Sukuk, that is cash generation. According to Ali (2009), this is the system from which the English concept of "Trust" was developed during the period of the Crusades.

Recent History of Sukuk in Islamic Capital Markets

In February 1988, during the fourth session of the Council of the Islamic Fiqh Academy in Jeddah, one of the very first descriptions of the modern-day Sukuk was issued. The description was under the heading of qiraad and muqarada, stating the ownership of investors in the shared asset (The Council of the Islamic Fiqh Academy, 1988). In 1990, Shell MDS published one of the first Sukuk in Malaysia (Dusuki, 2009). A number of institutions began issuing Sukuk from 2000 onwards and from there the Sukuk industry took off. In May 2003, the Accounting and Auditing Organization for

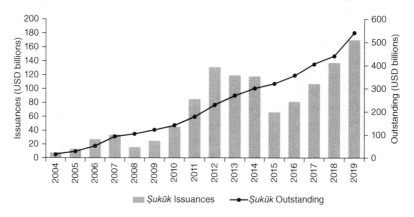

Figure 2.1 The development of Islamic capital markets through Sukuk issuance worldwide.

Source: (Islamic Financial Services Board, 2020)

Islamic Financial Institutions (AAOIFI) released its "Investment Sukuk" Shariah Standard No. 17 (Standards, 2003). The Sukuk market peaked in respect of issuance size in 2007. In 2008, a working paper was read by a prominent Islamic finance scholar, Muhammad Taqi Usmani, at the AAO-IFI conference, in which he declared that 80% of Sukuk structures are mere copies of interest-based systems (Usmani, 2007). As a result, the Sukuk market dropped from that peak. After that Ijarah Sukuk was introduced, which was more reliable as per Shariah Rulings. As a consequence of a resolution released by the AAOIFI in 2008, Sukuk al-ijara came to influence the Sukuk market from 2008 onwards due to a decline in equity-based Sukuk structures (Salah, 2014).

Sukuk Development in Different Countries

Reuters (2018) recorded an overall growth of 16% in 2017. Malaysia has been the leader in the Sukuk market since its recent inception. It issued the first Sukuk in 1990 and today it is the leader in the Sukuk market as per the volume and number of Sukuk issued. Through more than 60% of the outstanding global Sukuk (as of the end of 2009), Malaysia is the world's

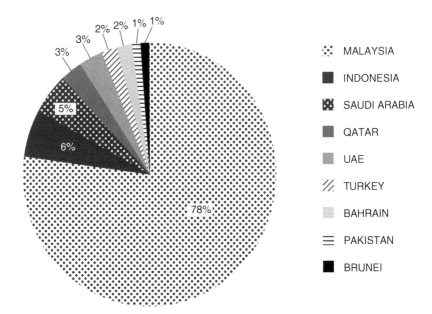

Figure 2.2 Share of Muslim countries in Sukuk development in the years 2001–2013
Source: (Smaoui & Khawaja, 2016)

largest Sukuk issuer. About 66.8% of the total Sukuk issued worldwide with a value of USD 67,872 million was issued on the Malaysian market, as presented in Table 1. The local currency Sukuk market stood at a whopping stage of USD 76.4 billion at the end of June 2010 (35.5% of the overall outstanding bond market) (Majid et al., 2012).

Recommendations were released by Bank Negara Malaysia, on 18 December 1993, on how a proposed Islamic interbank money market would work. The market started in Kuala Lumpur on 3 January 1994, with the primary purpose of encouraging interbank trade in Islamic financial instruments, especially Mudaraba Interbank Investments (MII). The MII structure offers a process by which an Islamic deficit banking institution (an investee bank) can receive funds from an Islamic surplus bank (an investor bank) by releasing a mudaraba certificate for a set investment term spanning from overnight to a year (Ahmad, 1997).

In December 2001, Cagamas Berhad, the Malaysian National Mortgage Company, launched a new framework for the acquisition of Islamic higher-purchase debt. This project and RHB Bank's launch of Islamic mutual funds focused on Sukuk holdings show how inventive Malaysia is when it comes to introducing new Islamic financial products (Wilson, 2004).

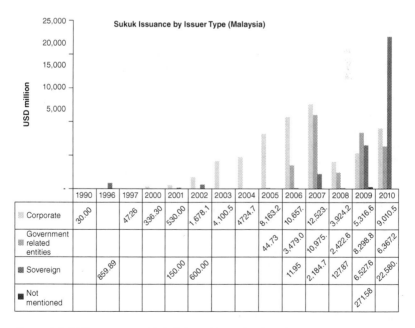

	1990	1996	1997	2000	2001	2002	2003	2004	2005	2006	2007	2008	2009	2010
Corporate	30.00		47.26	336.30	530.00	1,678.1	4,100.5	4724.7	8,163.2	10,657.	12,523.	3,924.2	5,316.6	9,010.5
Government related entities									44.73	3,479.0	10,975.	2,422.6	8,298.8	6,367.2
Sovereign		859.89			150.00	600.00			11,95	2,184.7		127.87	6,527.6	22,580.
Not mentioned													271.58	

Figure 2.3 Different types of Sukuk issued in Malaysia in history

Source: (RAM Rating Services Berhad, 2010)

All stakeholders of the market are now participating in Sukuk issuance in Malaysia, which clearly denotes.

Indonesia has been a vibrant country with Sukuk issuance after Malaysia, with 269 issuances in the period between 2003 and 2010 (Smaoui & Khawaja, 2016). It is followed by an Arab country, Bahrain, with 203 issuances within the same period. On 13 June 2001, the Bahrain Monetary Agency presented government bills designed to conform with Shari'a Islamic law for the first time in the Gulf. The bills were worth USD 25 million and in the shape of a three-month document known as Sukuk Salam securities (Wilson, 2004). The overall Bahrain-managed Sukuk portfolio surpassed USD 1 billion by October 2003 and the outlook for the years ahead looks very promising (Taskforce, 2003).

Qatar is one of the leaders in Islamic finance striving to become an Islamic finance hub in the region (Tlemsani, 2015). It owned over $81 billion of Islamic assets in the Islamic economy (Reuters, 2014). The biggest Sukuk of the industry was the Qatar Global Sukuk, estimated at USD 700 million and offered on 8 October 2003 that could be redeemed in 2010. UAE is also a huge market for Sukuk. According to Thomson Reuters (2018), it stood fourth in the total Sukuk assets, with over 31000 million dollars invested in this Islamic finance (IF) segment.

The first corporate Sukuk from Saudi Arabia was released in 2004 on behalf of HANCO Rent-A-Car, one of the largest car leasing and rental firms in the Kingdom. The stock, called the Caravan Sukuk, runs for a term of three years with a variable rate of return charged to buyers on a monthly basis, which is estimated to be 6% annually. Structured on an Ijarah basis, the Sukuk was authorized by Yasaar Limited, the supplier of advisory services to Shari'a, and operated by Volaw Trust and Corporate Services, a Jersey-based law firm with a presence in Jersey (Wilson, 2004). Then, on behalf of the National Central Cooling Company, which raised USD 100 million, a Sukuk called Tabreed was subsequently released, with the Sukuk structured using a mixture of Ijarah and istisna'a. The Foreign Investor of Kuwait and Credit Suisse First Boston were the lead executives (TradeArabia, 2004). Pakistan is also a prominent stakeholder in the global Sukuk market. A detailed deliberation on the development of Sukuk in Pakistan will be provided in the upcoming chapters.

Sukuk in Non-Muslim Countries

Biancone and Shakhatreh (2015) believe that most of the Non-Muslim countries do not have legislation that can apply to Islamic finance or Islamic securitization and that Islamic finance could be applied by using current laws to finance development projects. Islamic finance is not against non-Muslim societies, but its legal and equality concept is against the capitalist infrastructure. The governments of several non-Muslim European and Asian countries have demonstrated interest in the prospect of issuing Sukuk and a notable recent example of a Sukuk by a non-Muslim foreign borrower was the issue of a $500 million Sukuk Ltd. by GE Capital Sukuk Ltd. in November 2009 (Wedderburn-Day, 2010).

Reuters (2018) recorded that Hong Kong has 2000 million-dollar assets in Sukuk, followed by the United Kingdom by 1904 million dollars. Ivory Coast stood third in the fastest-growing countries as per Sukuk assets in 2017. It also revealed that European countries have issued 51 Sukuks with a volume of over 1500 million dollars. The Philippines executed its Islamic finance Act in 2016, which covers the Islamic capital market and Sukuk issuances also.

The report stated interesting stats about the Islamic finance education sector. The United Kingdom registered 76 certification institutes and 29-degree awarding institutes, more than any other country in the world. The United Kingdom is welcoming more Sukuk issuances and launching a regulation for this in near future (Miller et al., 2007).

Reflecting the consequences of the global financial crisis in the fall of 2008, the United Kingdom government declared that it had put on hold its intentions to release Sukuk. In July 2006, the first Sukuk was listed on the London Stock Exchange (Ainley et al., 2007).

Conventional Bond Market

With the concept of financial bonds and their typical operations in hand, it is necessary to discuss the structure and operations of a general bond market that is being operated globally. A bond market is essentially a financial market where conventional bonds of different types and associations are sold or bought by more than one party. The reason behind a separate identity of this market is the mere value of coupon and face amount of bond, which is interlinked with the liquidity ratios and other variations within this market. In this manner, different businesses, government financial institutions, and private individuals buy or sell bonds backed either by their businesses or by any authentic body. According to an approximation, if the collective size of the global bond market, in 2010, was estimated, its value can be reflected as standing at USD 82.2 trillion, with sellers and buyers ranging from government institutions to private individuals (Mccauley, 2009).

In these bond markets, different types of bonds and other financial security certificates are traded. Furthermore, the contributors of such markets range from government authorities, corporate investment firms, global and local traders of tangible and intangible products, to individuals – either as debt issuers or holders. A quick insight into demographics suggests that most of the global bond market is dominated by Western countries, especially by the United States, in which active bond markets have a volume of more than USD 343 billion that is 39% of the global bond market. This domination of the United States is followed by Japan, which has a contribution of 18% in global bond markets. Furthermore, other European and Asian countries such as France, Italy, the United Kingdom, China, and Russia also have a significant contribution to the rolling of the global bond market (Çelik et al., 2020).

Sukuk *Market*

Like a bond market, the Sukuk market is also a place where Sukuk holders and issuers are engaged with each other for trading these instruments. The global Sukuk market is not comparable to the enormous volume of the conventional bond market, but its growth rate and rapid penetration within Islamic and non-Islamic capital markets are an interesting case to be studied. At this stage, it is approximately calculated that the global Sukuk market has reached a significant size of USD 2 trillion in just a matter of few years – a growth rate that the conventional bond market has rarely seen in such a limited period. Furthermore, it is also predicted that, within the coming decade, the global Sukuk market's size would be crossing a benchmark of USD 4 trillion, which is a significant indication of how Sukuks are penetrating within global capital markets and their investors. According to El-Quqa et al. (2009), the major element behind this penetration and increased demand is the standardization of Islamic financial instruments, which has been carried out recently (as discussed in the Chapter 1). For supporting this claim, Hasan (2009) outlines that after the Islamic financing industry met its standardization codes by the year 2005, the global Sukuk market enjoyed a tremendous growth of 35% with major investors from countries such as Malaysia and UAE – a fact that was reported in the financial year of 2008. Furthermore, the global Muslim communities from regions such as the Middle East, Asia Pacific, and South Asia are continuing to align their business activities and market procedures with the newly standardized and Shariah approached Islamic financial model, which is also contributing to attraction elements within global Sukuk markets.

   In this regard, contribution toward the development of the global Sukuk market from different global regions is worth mentioning in this study. According to Hasan (2009), in countries such as Malaysia and UAE, *Sukuks* have now surpassed the domination of conventional bonds, and in only Malaysia, more than 40% of all bonds are *Sukuks*. Moreover, other Middle Eastern countries such as Kuwait, Qatar, Bahrain, Yemen, Oman, and

Saudi Arabia are also attracted by standardized *Sukuks,* and investors in these countries are now going for a Shariah-compliant Islamic bond, instead of conventional bonds. Moving toward the Asia Pacific and other GCC countries, it is worth noticing that their regional Sukuk market held USD 2.67 trillion in assets back in 2009, with a significant increase predicted in later years. This increased penetration of Sukuk is not only constrained with Islamic countries but many Western countries and their investors are also attracted by *Sukuks* and their benefits. For instance, multiple Western investors showed their deep interests in the Gulf Sukuk market, all because *Sukuks* have associated with their strong real value and low intrinsic risks. This is a fascinating approach outlined by Shariah, which has been explored recently – though, outlined abstractly some 1400 years ago. As a result of all this, the global bond market has been impacted seriously by the increased penetration of global Sukuk markets. According to Minas (2010), the total *Sukuks* issued in the first nine months of 2010 was equivalent to USD 27.9 billion, which was 62.3% more than what was witnessed in the first nine months of the financial year 2009. Furthermore, the global Sukuk market is also enjoying an average growth rate of 10–15% every year, for the last couple of years, which in a sense, is impacting and threatening the monopoly of global bond market in different Islamic and non-Islamic countries (El-Quqa et al., 2009; Minas, 2010). Further details for acceptance of *Sukuks* in different financial markets, along with their growing opportunities, are discussed in the next chapter.

References

Ahmad, A. (1997). *Towards an Islamic financial market: A study of Islamic banking and finance in Malaysia.* Research Paper No. 45. Islamic Research and Training Institute – Islamic Development Bank.

Ainley, M., Mashayekhi, A., Hicks, R., Rahman, A., & Ravalia, A. (2007, November). Islamic finance in the UK: Regulation and challenges. *The Financial Services Authority, 36.* http://ara.assaif.org/content/download/279/3459/file/Islamic Finance in the UK.pdf

Ali, I. B. (2009). *Waqf: A sustainable development institution for Muslim communities.* Takaaful T&T Friendly Society. www.takaafultt.org

Al Qurtabi, S. B. K. (2008). *Al Muntaqa explanation of Al Muwatta.* Maktabah As Sa'adah.

Berber, M. A. (2014). *From interest to usury: The transformation of Murābaha in the late Ottoman Empire.* İstanbul Şehir University.

Biancone, P. P., & Shakhatreh, M. Z. (2015). Using Islamic finance for infrastructure projects in non-Muslim countries. *European Journal of Islamic Finance, 2,* 1–9.

Braudel, F. (1995). *The Mediterranean and the Mediterranean world in the age of Philip II* (Vol. 2). University of California Press.

Çelik, S., Demirtas, G., & Isaksson, M. (2020). *Corporate bond market trends, emerging risks and monetary policy.* OECD Capital Market Series. http://www.oecd.org

Cizakca, M. (2010). *Domestic borrowing without the rate of interest: Gharar and the origins of sukuk.* University Library of Munich.

The Council of the Islamic Fiqh Academy. (1988). *Resolution no. 30 (5/4): Muqaradha bonds and investment certificates.* Council of the Islamic Fiqh Academy.

Dusuki, A. W. (2009). *Challenges of realizing Maqasid Al-shari'ah (objectives of Shari'ah) in the Islamic capital market: Special focus on equity-based sukuk structures.* International Shari'ah Research Academy for Islamic Finance (ISRA).

El-Quqa, O. M., Hasan, F., Alsahli, K., & Ahmed, N. (2009). *Sukuk market – down but not out.* MENA Sukuk Report. Global Investment House.

Hasan, F. (2009). *Global sukuk market.* Global Investment House Research Archives.

Jaffer, S. (2004). *Islamic asset management: Forming the future for Shari'a-compliant investment strategies.* Euromoney Books.

Khan, M. A., & Watson, T. (2003). *Islamic economics and finance: A glossary.* Routledge.

Majid, H. A., Shahimi, S., & Abdullah, M. H. S. B. (2012). Sukuk defaults and its implication: A case study of Malaysian capital market. In *8th international conference on Islamic economics and finance sukuk* (pp. 1–37). Center for Islamic Economics and Finance, Qatar Faculty of Islamic Studies, Qatar Foundation Access.

Mccauley, R. (2009). *International banking and financial market developments.* Bank for International Settlements.

Miller, N. D., Challoner, J., & Atta, A. (2007). UK welcomes the sukuk-how the UK finance bill should stimulate Islamic finance in London, much to the delight of the City's banks. *International Financial Law Review, 26,* 24.

Minas, Q. J. (2010). Prospects for sukuk market brighter. *The Saudi Gazette.*

Mohammed, N. (2014). *Sukuk: An introduction to the underlying principles and structure.* https://www.sukuk.com/education/sukuk-introduction-underlying-principles-structure-277/#/?playlistId=0&videoId=0

RAM Rating Services Berhad. (2010). *RAM ratings sukuk focus.* http://www.sc.com.my/paper.asp%0A?pageid=603&menuid=&newsid=&year=2009

Reuters, I. (2014). *Islamic finance development report 2017 towards sustainability.* Islamic Finance Development.

Salah, O. (2014). Development of sukuk: Pragmatic and idealist approaches to sukuk structures. *Journal of International Banking Law and Regulation, 1,* 41–52.

Schoon, N. (2009). *Islamic banking and finance.* Spiramus Press Ltd.

Smaoui, H., & Khawaja, M. (2016, November). The determinants of sukuk market development. *Emerging Markets Finance and Trade.* https://doi.org/10.1080/1540496X.2016.1224175

Standards, A. S. (2003). *Investment sukuk.* AAOIF.

Taskforce, I. B. T. (2003, October). Billion dollar sukuk portfolio for Bahrain. *Islamic Banking Hub Quarterly, 1.*

Thomson Reuters. (2018). *Islamic finance development report.* https://ceif.iba.edu.pk/pdf/Reuters-Islamic-finance-development-report2018.pdf

Tlemsani, I. (2015). Qatar as an emerging Islamic finance hub. *Journal of Modern Accounting and Auditing, 11*(11), 596–605. https://doi.org/10.17265/1548-6583/2015.11.004

TradeArabia. (2004, April 12). Capital market news. *TradeArabia.*

Usmani, M. T. (2007). *Sukuk and their contemporary applications* (DeLorenzo, T. S. Y., Trans. from the original Arabic). AAOIFI Shari'a Council Meeting.

Vallely, P. (2006). How Islamic inventors changed the world. *The Independent, 11.*

Wedderburn-Day, A. R. (2010). Sovereign "sukuk": Adaptation and innovation. *Law and Contemporary Problems, 73*(4), 325–333.

Wilson, R. (2004). Overview of the sukuk market. In *Islamic bonds: Your guide to issuing, structuring and investing in sukuk* (pp. 6–7). Euromoney Books.

3 Differentiating Between Conventional Bonds and Sukuks

Rabia Sabri, Imam Uddin, Muhammad AsadUllah, Muhammad Omer Rafique, and M. Ishaq Bhatti

Introduction

This chapter is intended to provide brief details regarding conventional bonds and their structures, historical timeline, and their categories issued in different international markets (including Pakistan). Furthermore, this chapter (through a discussion of conventional bonds and their respective details) seeks to clarify and develop a difference between conventional bonds and Islamic *Sukuks* – a topic that has remained under debate in international Islamic finance markets. In this manner, after the difference between these instruments is clarified, this study will move forward toward identifying the growth opportunities for Sukuk in different Islamic capital markets around the globe.

Financial Bonds

In conventional financing markets, a bond is regarded as a formal contract between its issuer and holder, in which the issuer owes the holder a debt to be repaid with interest at a mutually agreed date in the later time (O'Sullivan et al., 2003). In other words, these are debt security certificates that oblige the issuer to pay the debt amount to the holder with interest either at fixed intervals or at once in the future. According to De Haan and Hinloopen (2003), the subsequent details and study of these financial debt certificates reveal that these can be regarded as a category of financial loans as well, in which, the issuer becomes the borrower of money and the holder serves as its lender, and a coupon for this money becomes the interest. In a nutshell, this is a very broad and wide topic that is to be covered briefly in the coming sub-sections of this chapter in order to explore any possible correlations or differences between these certificates and *Sukuks* (beside the exclusion of Riba from *Sukuks*).

DOI: 10.4324/9781003243755-3

Features of Financial Bonds

There are some universally agreed intrinsic and extrinsic features of conventional financial bonds (Parameswaran, 2011). Here we present a gist of these basic features to compare the crust of conventional bond with Sukuk. These can be summarized as follows:

1   A financial bond has associated with it a face amount, which can be described as an amount on which the issuer pays interest, and which (in most cases) has to be repaid at the end of the term.
2   A conventional financial bond has associated with it an issue price, which is a price at which an investor or holder buys the bond upon their first-time issuance. The amount of this price is approximately equal to the face amount in many cases if issuance fees and net proceeds are excluded.
3   A typical conventional bond has associated with it a maturity date, which refers to the date at which the issuer has to repay the face amount. This maturity date is counted after the exact day of issuance

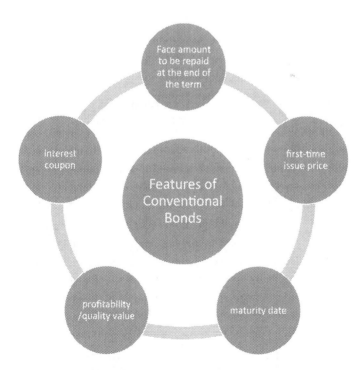

Figure 3.1 Features of financial bonds

of financial bonds to investors and can be varied from few months to multiple years.

4   A typical conventional bond has associated with it a coupon that is formally known as the interest value that issuer pays to the bondholders, and can be of fixed and variable nature, depending upon the type of bond issued.

5   A conventional bond has associated with a quality value, which determines the profitability it will attain for the holding investor.

Besides these universally approved and features of conventional bonds, there are also some other features that are subject to variation in their order or existence in different bond types. These features include putability of a bond (i.e. power of investor to force the issuer to repay the bond's value before the maturity date), callability of a bond (i.e. power of the issuer to pay back the value of a bond even before the maturity date), the optionality of a bond (i.e. right of reselling the bond within a specified frame of time for either holder or issuer), and many others (Brennan & Schwartz, 1977; Geske & Johnson, 1984; Pye, 1975).

Types of Conventional Bonds

For a quick consideration, some most commonly available and applicable types of bonds in the international bond market are listed as follows (Richelson & Richelson, 2011):

1   Fixed-Rate Bonds: These conventional bonds have with them a coupon (i.e. the interest value) which remains fixed throughout the pre-determined life of a financial bond.

2   Zero-Coupon Bonds: These types of financial bonds have no fixed coupon value associated with them, and this coupon value is expected to be rolled up as the bond approaches its maturity date. Moreover, these bonds can be sold out in such a way that their coupon value and original bond value could be traded separately.

3   Asset-Backed Bonds: These are types of conventional bonds in which coupon value (i.e. interest) and face amount (i.e. principal amount) are subject to be associated or backed up with the underlying cash flows from other assets and their values.

4   Treasury Bonds: These types of financial bonds are also known as government bonds with the lowest interest rates since they are only issued by the legal state-owned financing authorities.

5   Corporate Bonds: These are typically the type of bonds, which are issued by private corporations which seek to raise their capital for corporate expansion.

6   Convertible Bonds: These types of conventional bonds can be converted into shares of common stock or cash under the maturity period, at a mutually agreed value between issuer and holder.

7   Linker Bonds: These types of conventional bonds have their face amount and coupon value associated with the variable inflation rate.

8   Perpetual Bonds: These are special types of conventional bonds which have no particular maturity date associated with them.

9   Subordinated Bonds: These types of conventional bonds are identified by the feature that their priority becomes low at the time of liquidity of its issuer.

Conventional Bonds and *Sukuks*

At this stage, it should be clarified in a succinct manner that what are the core differences between conventional financial bonds and Sukuk certificates, except that the second one does not employ Riba in its structural identity. For this, we can summarize the previously mentioned details regarding both *Sukuks* and conventional bonds to explore the differences further. In a nutshell, a conventional financial bond (of any type) is a security certificate in the form of a debt that is to be paid back before a certain date (i.e. maturity date) along with the interest that is coupon value or simply, Riba. In a more precise manner, a bond is debt security under which the borrowed money against a bond certificate is to be paid back with a fixed or variable interest. However, *Sukuks* are financial fixed income certificates that are raised on trading or any other specifically identifiable and legitimate legal asset. The key point which is to be observed over here is highlighted by Al-Nasser (2009) that bonds are proof of debt, while *Sukuks* are proof of ownership.

Furthermore, bonds have with them a fixed rate of interest regardless of loss or gain, while money in return for *Sukuks* is associated with a genuine legal contract between Sukuk issuer and holder. In an even broader sense, bonds are subject to expiry at a pre-determined value, while *Sukuks* only expire at either their market value that is a pre-arranged and agreed figure or a fair (profit/loss bearing) value (Al-Nasser, 2009). In contrast to these differences, there are some similarities between *Sukuks* and formal conventional bonds as well. According to a report compiled by *Dar Al-Istithmar* in 2006, both *Sukuks* and conventional bonds can be marketed (i.e. both instruments are liquid, easily transferable, and tradable), rate-able (i.e. both of them can be easily rated), enhance-able (i.e. both of them in different formats allow for credit enhancements), and versatile (i.e. both of multiple structures and types currently in practice) (Al Istithmar, 2006).

Table 3.1 Differences between Bonds and Sukuk

	Bonds	Sukuk
Base of the instrument	Traditional bonds are debt-based.	Sukuk must be, backed by (asset-backed Sukuk) cash, ventures, and/or economic operations, unlike
Asset ownership	Bonds do not offer a share of ownership to the investor in the asset, project, business, or joint venture they fund. That is a loan duty from the borrower to the buyer of the note.	Sukuk gives partial ownership to the investor in the asset on which Sukuk is based.
Investment criteria	Bonds may typically be used to fund any asset, project, company, or joint venture that complies with local laws.	The property on which Sukuk is based must be sharia-compliant.
Issue unit	A share of the debt is expressed by each bond.	A share of the underlying asset reflects each Sukuk.
Investment rewards and risks	For the life of the bond, bondholders earn regularly scheduled (and sometimes fixed rate) interest payments and their principal is expected to be repaid at the maturity date of the bond.	A share of income from the underlying asset is earned by Sukuk holders (and accept a share of any loss incurred).
Issue price	The face value of a bond price is dependent on the credit worthiness of the issuer (including its rating).	Sukuk's face value is dependent on the market value of the underlying asset.
Effects of costs	In general, bond investors are not affected by costs associated with the asset, project, business, or joint venture they fund. Investor incentives are not influenced by the performance of the underlying asset.	Sukuk investors are impacted by the underlying asset-related costs. Higher costs can result in lower profits for investors and vice versa.
Sale of instrument	Bond sales are the selling of loans.	When you sell the Sukuk, you sell ownership of the assets that support them.
Rate of return	The return is pre-determined in the case of Bonds.	The return in the case of Sukuk is "expected return."
Major risk	The major risk (credit risk) in the case of traditional bonds lies with the bond issuer.	As far as risk management is concerned, the main risk in the case of Sukuk lies with the underlying assets.

For details and pieces of evidence of the structural and impactful differences mentioned earlier, see Afshar (2013), Alam et al. (2013), Cakir & Raei (2007), Fathurahman & Fitriati (2013), Ramasamy & Shanmugam Munisamy (2011), and Safari (2011).

Risks in Sukuk

The certificate holder is rendered to several risks pertinent to Sukuk structures. These risks hinder the productivity and popularity of these instruments. Various measures are being taken to overcome these risks, but some of them are embedded in these structures, which in fact are distinguishing lines between conventional and Shariah-complaint arrangements. The risks are as follows.

Rate of Return Risk

Sukuk is subject to this risk dependent on fixed rates in the same way as fixed-rate bonds are exposed to interest-rate risk. The increase in market interest rates is contributing to a decline in the valuation of Sukuk fixed income. Through widespread benchmarking with Karachi Inter-Bank Offering Rate (KIBOR) in their funding activities, Sukuk certificates are implicitly vulnerable to interest rate fluctuations (Nanaeva, 2010).

Risk of Loss of Asset

Numerous risks often refer to the underlying properties of the Sukuk certificates. Primarily, the possibility of a loss of assets is present. Islamic finance, however in the context of Takaful, has Shariah-compliant guidelines for insurance claims, and these arrangements would have to be used to mitigate the costs of asset losses (Tariq & Dar, 2007).

Foreign Exchange-Rate Risks

Currency vulnerability comes from adverse fluctuations in exchange rates, which would undeniably have an impact on foreign exchange positions. In the case of a divergence between the unit of currency in which the securities are denominated in the Sukuk pool and the denominational currency in which the Sukuk funds are deposited, the exchange-rate liability is allocated to the Sukuk holders (Tariq, 2004).

Credit Risk

Credit risk refers to the possibility of an asset or debt being irrecoverable due to a default or settlement pause (Duffie & Singleton, 2012). Due to the prohibition of interest, debt rescheduling at a higher markup rate is not necessary. Therefore, the investor has to bear this risk.

Default Risk

Traditional bonds are a debt obligation, Sukuk is a certificate of ownership, so the probability of retrieving their original investment is very minimal in the event of default. Only within the scope of their power and skills will the Sukuk managers be responsible for any Sukuk default. Therefore, all risks under Sukuk would be absorbed by Sukuk holders if default happens due to external variables, such as "force major" or global financial crisis (Nanaeva, 2010). This issue may be solved through the formation of an Islamic Rating Agency. This will decline the probability of default to minimal.

Shariah Compliance Risk

The risk of Shariah compliance is a risk related only to Islamic resources. It is defined as a risk of asset value loss due to the incompliance of Sukuk with Shariah values (DeLorenzo, 2006). Each Sukuk issue should be endorsed as compliant with Islamic decisions by the Shariah board. In light of criticism by some Shariah scholars regarding the non-Islamic character of most modern Sukuk, this form of risk has become quite relevant (Usmani, 2007).

Liquidity Risk

For Islamic finance in general and Sukuk in particular, liquidity risk is critical. Due to Shariah prohibitions on the trading in debt and other shares, IFIs have restricted instruments to handle their liquidity. Short-term inter-bank loans and last resort loans from the Central Bank are not applicable to Islamic banks because of the ban on Riba. Certificates of Sukuk are listed on many local exchanges, but their liquidity is not expressed by this alone. Their continued performance would ultimately depend on their ability to mature into highly liquid funds with sufficient risk management mechanisms (Tariq & Dar, 2007).

References

Afshar, T. A. (2013). Compare and contrast sukuk (Islamic Bonds) with conventional bonds, are they compatible? *Journal of Global Business Management, 9*(1), 44.
Alam, N., Hassan, M. K., & Haque, M. A. (2013). Are Islamic bonds different from conventional bonds? International evidence from capital market tests. *Borsa Istanbul Review, 13*(3), 22–29.

Al Istithmar, D. (2006). *Sukuk-an introduction to the underlying principles and structure*. Dar Al Istithmar Ltd. Retrieved October 24, 2013.

Al-Nasser, L. (2009). *The difference between sukuk and bonds*. Gulf Business Intelligence.

Brennan, M. J., & Schwartz, E. S. (1977). Savings bonds, retractable bonds and callable bonds. *Journal of Financial Economics*, 5(1), 67–88.

Cakir, S., & Raei, F. (2007). *Sukuk vs. Eurobonds: Is there a difference in value-at-risk?* IMF Working Papers (pp. 1–20). IMF.

De Haan, L., & Hinloopen, J. (2003). Preference hierarchies for internal finance, bank loans, bond, and share issues: Evidence for Dutch firms. *Journal of Empirical Finance*, 10(5), 661–681.

DeLorenzo, T. S. Y. (2006). Shari'ah compliance risk. *Chicago Journal of International Law*, 7, 397.

Duffie, D., & Singleton, K. J. (2012). *Credit risk: Pricing, measurement, and management*. Princeton University Press.

Fathurahman, H., & Fitriati, R. (2013). Comparative analysis of return on sukuk and conventional bonds. *American Journal of Economics*, 3(3), 159–163.

Geske, R., & Johnson, H. E. (1984). The American put option valued analytically. *The Journal of Finance*, 39(5), 1511–1524.

Nanaeva, Z. (2010, May). *How risky sukuk are: Comparative analysis of risks associated with sukuk and conventional bonds* المقارن بيه بالصكوك والسندات التقليدية تتمثل خطورة الصكوك في التحليل [Dissertation submitted in partial fulfillment, University of Portsmouth].

O'Sullivan, A., Sheffrin, S. M., & Perez, S. J. (2003). *Instructor's manual, macroeconomics: Principles and tools*. Pearson Education.

Parameswaran, S. (2011). *Fundamentals of financial instruments: An introduction to stocks, bonds, foreign exchange, and derivatives*. John Wiley & Sons.

Pye, G. (1975). The value of the call option on a bond. In *Stochastic optimization models in finance* (pp. 547–552). Elsevier.

Ramasamy, R., & Shanmugam Munisamy, M. H. (2011). Relative risk of Islamic sukuk over government and conventional bonds. *Global Journal of Management and Business Research*, 11(6).

Richelson, H., & Richelson, S. (2011). *Bonds: The unbeaten path to secure investment growth* (Vol. 145). John Wiley & Sons.

Safari, M. (2011). *Are sukuk securities the same as conventional bonds?* Proceedings of Foundation of Islamic Finance Series, Second Conference.

Tariq, A. A. (2004, September). *Managing financial risks of sukuk structures*. Loughborough University (mimeo).

Tariq, A. A., & Dar, H. (2007, April). Risks of sukuk structures: Implications for resource mobilization. *Thunderbird International Business Review*, 49, 203–223. https://doi.org/10.1002/tie

Usmani, M. T. (2007). *Sukuk and their contemporary applications* (DeLorenzo, T. S. Y., Trans. from the original Arabic). AAOIFI Shari'a Council Meeting.

4 Shariah Perspective on Sukuk

Imam Uddin, Muhammad Omer Rafique,
Rabia Sabri, Muhammad AsadUllah, and
M. Ishaq Bhatti

Introduction

This chapter deliberates the Shariah debate on the topic of issuing and earning from Sukuk. Firstly, the chapter outlines the basic Shariah features and characteristics of Sukuk and then defines the opinion of Sharia scholars regarding the legitimacy of Sukuk. The author has also summarized the critical Shariah points in the process of issuing an earning from the Sukuk structures, which have been the crux of critics from Shariah scholars. The criticism of prominent Shariah scholars had a negative impact on the global Sukuk market; therefore, this criticism is vital to address in order to mitigate the Sharia risk in structuring the Sukuk.

Key Characteristics of *Sukuk*

The Sukuk in its modern-day characteristics shares remarkable similarities with the Ottoman concepts of *Waqf* and *Esham* in its operational framework. According to a formal client note prepared by Hogan Lovells Law Firm (2004), the Sukuk represents proportionate beneficial ownership and may be described as an Islamic bond. In its operations, the risk and return associated with cash flows are generated by a particular asset belonging to investors (also known as Sukuk holders), for a defined domain of time. Some of the key characteristics of these modern-day Sukuk are listed as follows:

1   Sukuk, in its equal value, is a document or financial certificate issued either in the name of its owner or of the bearer, to enact the right of ownership of representation.
2   These certificates present a common share of ownership of assets (non-monetary, usufructs, tangible and usufructs, monetary assets, etc.) available for investment.
3   A Sukuk document does not represent a financial obligation (or debt) indebted to the issuer by the Sukuk holder.

DOI: 10.4324/9781003243755-4

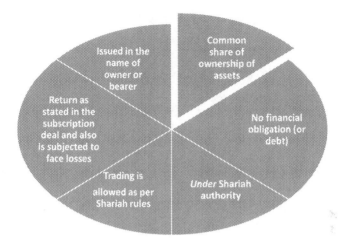

Figure 4.1 Key characteristics of Sukuk

4   *Sukuks* are issued within the regulation of a Shariah authority, which also governs its trading procedures.
5   Trading of these certificates is subject to the terms that govern the trading of the rights they represent.
6   The owner of Sukuk certificates is subjected to share the return as stated in the subscription deal and also is subjected to face losses – according to the share of his or her ownership.

Shariah Perspectives

Sukuk is presented as a Shariah-compliant investment product. It is of utmost importance that it should be complying all the rules of Shariah, rather it would be mis-representation. This is a debatable topic; researchers have written a lot on this topic.

To take a bird's eye view we present some major Shariah perspectives regarding issuance, operations, and functions of *Sukuks*, mutually agreed by Shariah boards of different Islamic countries can be briefly outlined as follows:

1   *Sukuks* can be issued over the permission of the respective Shariah board if their subscription is made for investment.
2   *Sukuks* can be issued for securities of trading in tangible assets and usufructs by partitioning these assets or usufructs into units of equivalent

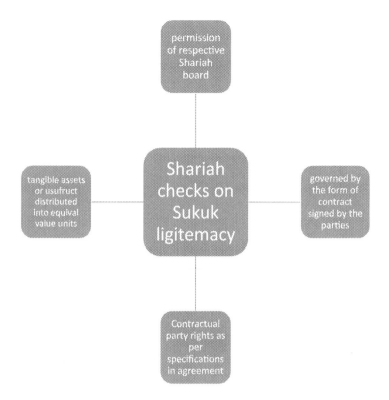

Figure 4.2 Major Shariah perspectives on Sukuks

value and then issuing securities representing respective values. However, *Sukuks* cannot be issued for maintaining securities for receivables.

3   The contract of issuance of Sukuk certificates is to be governed according to the specifications made at the time of agreement between parties, after closing and issuance dates. These parties are to be called issuers and subscribers in a legal manner.

4   The relationship between two parties within a contract can be ascertained as per the contract that serves as the basis of the issue between them.

5   The relationship between issuer and subscriber is to be governed by applicable contracts for issuing Sukuk certificates.

In short, *Sukuks* can be outlined as fixed income securities, which are investments providing capital returns in the format of fixed payments leading to the eventual return of the principal amount (at the time of agreement maturity). For this Shariah not only holds legal, legitimate but also makes it clear that these securities should not be debt-based, or otherwise, they will be termed as Riba included, which is strictly forbidden in the Islamic code of business conduct. Also, the Shariah perspective outlines that any loan which is given out on interest or mark-up invites the curse of Almighty Allah and, thus, is strictly prohibited and illegitimate. This concept can be marked as the motivator for the development and growth of Sukuk in most of the Islamic countries.

Shariah Critical Points in Sukuk

Many Shariah scholars have written on the Shariah legitimacy of these Sukuk and pointed out several gaps as per Shariah rulings in different structures. Thus, from issuance till maturity every step should be planned as per Shariah rulings. Some of these critical Shariah points are compiled as follows.

Figure 4.3 Sukuk Shariah critical points
Source: Fathurahman and Fitriati (2013)

Beneficial Ownership in Asset-Based Sukuk

Real Ownership of Sukuk is a question in almost all structures. Especially in the asset-based Sukuk structures, the ownership of assets is only of beneficial nature with no real rights of any ownership. Therefore most asset-based Sukuk pictures are not approved by Shariah boards.

Recourse to the Underlying Assets in Sukuk

If there is a default in payments, Sukuk holders can turn to the debtor (originator). This recourse is questioned by many Shariah scholars because the promise of this recourse makes the Sukuk similar to an interest-earning contract.

Foregoing One's Rights (Tanazul)

This is an essential arrangement done by some of the Sukuk structures, in which the owner forgoes his right of getting the real profit share and settle on an agreed profit capped in the master agreement.

Purchase Undertaking (Wa'ad)

Howladar (2009) commented that almost in all asset-based systems to date, purchasing undertaking arrangements are central. This process is used to refund principal to the Sukuk holders and is normally a deal that "obliges" the originator to "buy" back the properties at par value (i.e. irrespective of the "true" realizable asset value) (often with a related sales undertaking).

Rebate (Ibra') in Sale-Based Sukuk

The seller of the Sukuk agrees to rebate the buyer in a sale-based Sukuk and not charge him an amount more than the capped return. This condition in any contract is not Sharia-compliant. It was prohibited by Prophet peace be upon him, he did not allow a rebate to the purchaser in the condition when he agrees to pay an amount before the maturity.

Liquidity Facility in the Event of a Shortfall in Musharakah Sukuk

Musharakah Sukuk denotes the ownership of Sukuk holders in the underlying asset. The pre-contract or in contract promise of selling the Sukuk back to the Special Purpose Vehicle (SPV) makes this Musharaka Sukuk non-Sharia compliant.

Tradability of Sale-Based Sukuk

Any Sukuk where the Sukuk holders do not enjoy ownership in the underlying asset, these Sukuk cannot be tradeable in the secondary market because they represent only receivables, trading them in the secondary market means a trade of debts, which is explicitly prohibited by Prophet SAW.

Portfolio of Asset as Sukuk Underlying Asset

Accounting and Auditing Organization for Islamic Financial Institutions (AAOIFI) has also identified several pitfalls of issuing and structuring Sukuk. Among them is the principle that "To be tradable, Sukuk should not be backed solely by receivables and Sukuk profit should not be supported by the mudarib (usually the borrower)" (Standards, 2003).

Shariah Critique on Sukuk Structures

It was reported that, in 2008, a statement was released in November 2007 by Shaikh Muhammad Taqi Usmani, Chairman of the AAOIFI Shariah Board, saying that up to 85% of the Sukuk issued so far could not have been completely compliant with Shariah (Usmani, 2007). This caused a negative

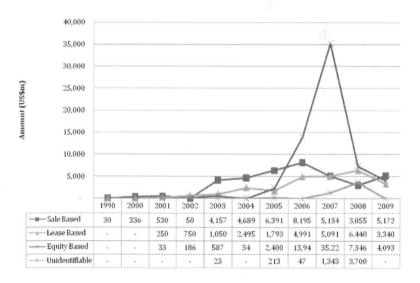

	1990	2000	2001	2002	2003	2004	2005	2006	2007	2008	2009
Sale Based	30	336	530	50	4,157	4,689	6,391	8,195	5,134	3,055	5,172
Lease Based	-	-	250	750	1,050	2,495	1,793	4,991	5,091	6,440	3,340
Equity Based	-	-	33	186	587	34	2,400	13,94	35,22	7,346	4,093
Unidentifiable	-	-	-	-	23	-	213	47	1,343	3,700	-

Figure 4.4 Fall in equity-based Sukuk after the Shariah critique

Source: (Dusuki, 2009)

impact on the global Sukuk market, especially in the equity-based category and the industry witnessed a slump. It was argued that the slump was due to the global financial crisis, but the negative impact of this criticism cannot be overlooked.

Dusuki (2010) illustrates some of the asset-based Sukuk's Shariah problems:

- The inconsistency between legal documents and the need for Shariah: The legal documents do not reveal the ownership and Qabz (the real possession) of Sukuk holders (Dusuki & Mokhtar, 2010).
- The owners of Sukuk do not have the right to sell the underlying land.
- The use of wa'ad (purchase enterprise) in Sukuk is dependent on equity. The promise is considered as part of the contract.
- The independence of SPV: In most matters like rating and credit ranking, SPV is not considered a separate entity.

Hidayat (2013) concluded that the asset-backed Sukuk structure is considered to be more Shariah-compliant in type and content than the asset-based framework. Aziz et al. (2013) presented a detailed study on the Maqasid-e-Shariah paradigms to be considered as decisive in the legitimacy of a particular Sukuk. The analysis also involves Maslahah and Sadd-e-Zarae checks to be applied on the same. Ahmed et al. (2019) listed some determinants for the legitimacy of a particular Sukuk. The determinants list includes:

- type of Sukuk structure,
- Shariah auditing,
- Shariah risk, and
- Shariah documentation.

The Shariah compliance risk is one of the significant rudiments that may have an influence on the Sukuk legitimacy (E. R. Ahmed, 2015). A negative association between the risks of Shariah complaints and the validity of Sukuk, suggesting the major influence of the risks of Shariah complaints on increasing legitimacy.

A major issue faced by *Sukuks* in many Islamic countries is the non-standardized and non-uniformed procedures taken by Shariah boards due to unsettled ideological and sectarian believes associated with financing and other transactions (E. W. M. Ahmed, 2007). Bukhari et al. (2014) analyzed several Sukuk structures and revealed that the essential notion of an interest-free market in issuing Sukuk was not thoroughly realized.

Therefore, Shariah legitimacy is a core point of concern that participates in the success of the Sukuk in the market. We will deliberate this point further in the upcoming chapters of Sukuk structures.

References

Ahmed, E. R. (2015, May). An empirical analysis on legitimacy of sukuk: An insight of Malaysian sukuk. *Asian Social Science, 11*(13). https://doi.org/10.5539/ass.v11n13p84

Ahmed, E. R., Islam, A., & Amran, A. B. (2019). Examining the legitimacy of sukuk structure via shariah pronouncements. *Journal of Islamic Marketing, 10*(4), 1151–1166. https://doi.org/10.1108/JIMA-03-2018-0050

Ahmed, E. W. M. (2007). Sukuk – a sharia advisory perspective. *Islamic Finance News, 4.*

Aziz, M. R. A., Shahid, M. F. I., & Ibrahim, M. F. (2013, September). The structure of sukuk ijarah: An initial analysis from the perspective of Maqasid Al-Shariah. *Paper Proceeding of the 5th Islamic Economics System Conference (IECONS 2013), Sustainable*, 4–5.

Bukhari, S. M. H., Nawaz, H., & Sair, A. (2014). Compliance of investment sukuk with shariah. *Science International (Lahore), 26*(4), 1697–1706.

Dusuki, A. W. (2009). *Challenges of realizing Maqasid Al-shari'ah (objectives of Shari'ah) in the Islamic capital market: Special focus on equity-based sukuk structures.* International Shari'ah Research Academy for Islamic Finance (ISRA).

Dusuki, A. W. (2010). Do equity-based sukuk structures in Islamic capital markets manifest the objectives of shariah? *Journal of Financial Services Marketing, 15*(3), 203–214. https://doi.org/10.1057/fsm.2010.17

Dusuki, A. W., & Mokhtar, S. (2010). *Critical appraisal of shariah issues on ownership in asset-based sukuk as implemented in the Islamic debt market.* International Shari'ah Research Academy for Islamic Finance (ISRA).

Fathurahman, H., & Fitriati, R. (2013). Comparative analysis of return on sukuk and conventional bonds. *American Journal of Economics, 3*(3), 159–163.

Hidayat, S. E. (2013). A comparative analysis between asset based and asset backed sukuk: Which one is more shariah compliant. *International SAMANM Journal of Finance and Accounting, 1*(2), 24–31.

Hogan Lovells Law Firm. (2004). *Islamic finance: Shariah, sukuk & securitization.* Hogan Lovells Law Firm.

Howladar, K. (2009). *The future of sukuk: Substance over form?* Durham University Press.

Standards, A. S. (2003). *Investment sukuk.* Sharia Standard.

Usmani, M. T. (2007). *Sukuk and their contemporary applications* (DeLorenzo, T. S. Y., Trans. from the original Arabic). AAOIFI Shari'a Council Meeting.

5 Common Structures of Sukuk

Rabia Sabri, Imam Uddin, Muhammad Omer Rafique, Muhammad AsadUllah, and M. Ishaq Bhatti

Introduction

This chapter outlines some of the most commonly employed structures of Sukuk, which have been proposed in detail by the Accounting and Auditing Organization for Islamic Financial Institutions (AAOIFI) in the year 2002. Through explaining these structures, this study would be approaching the variations and formats that *Sukuks* have acquired in the modern financial and capital markets. Moreover, this handbook would be presenting to its readers the idea of how *Sukuks* could be used in different corporate scenarios and financial products, in connection to the previous chapter, for confirming the assertion regarding future opportunities which await this wonderful development. It will conclude with a brief discussion regarding legal issues and limitations for the *Sukuks* in capital markets, giving way for this study to move toward its finalizing sections.

AAOIFI-Proposed Common Structures of Sukuk

Presented in the following lines are the details of some major structures of *Sukuk*, as outlined by AAOIFI in its 2002 recommendations, which are explained in a report compiled by *Dar Ul Istithmar's* whitepaper. Each structure is first explained briefly and is followed by its diagrammatic illustration and interpretation, along with its implementation and practicing procedure:

Sukuk Al-Ijarah *(Lease-Based Sukuks)*

The basic Ijarah Sukuk is an issuance of securities where the core transaction between the issuer and obligor requires a lease of tangible property. This is the most commonly employed Sukuk structure in the current Islamic finance industry. In Islamic finance terminology, *Ijarah* is a contract between two parties with which one party leases any equipment or asset from the second party

DOI: 10.4324/9781003243755-5

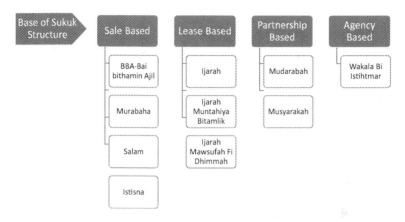

Figure 5.1 Different types of Sukuk structures

on a rental basis. In this type of contract, the ownership of the equipment or asset remains with the leasing party until full payment is made in rent, within a pre-defined domain of time. Therefore, *Sukuk Al-Ijarah* is securities of defined and existing equipment or assets which are bounded under a contract of lease or *Ijarah* and can be traded in the market at a fixed rate. According to experts, *Sukuk Al-Ijarah* is vulnerable to risks associated with the ability and desirability of the second party to pay the rents (Lahsasna et al., 2018b). Furthermore, these types of securities do not always involve fixed and expected net return as determined at the time of issuance, all because the leased item could develop some sort of serious malfunctioning not addressed at the time of agreement. However, these types of *Sukuks* offer a high degree of flexibility concerning marketability and issuance frequency. Moreover, their issuance could take place either from the financial institutions or simply from the holder of the leased item (Lahsasna et al., 2018a).

The structure of Sukuk *Al-Ijarah* can be illustrated as follows:

In the above illustration, the structure of *Sukuk Al-Ijarah* is explained as follows: The obligator sells certain assets to the special purpose entity (can be a corporation, individual, etc.) at a pre-determined price, after which, this entity issues *Sukuk Al-Ijarah* certificates equivalent to the amount of pre-determined price of the sold asset and passes it to the obligator as a seller. At this stage, an *Ijarah* agreement is formed between a special purpose entity and the obligator over a pre-defined period of time, and the obligator tends to lease back the asset as a lessee. In this manner, the special purpose entity receives monthly rentals from the obligator and distributes them accordingly to the Sukuk holders (Rohmatunnisa, 2008). Finally, at the stage of

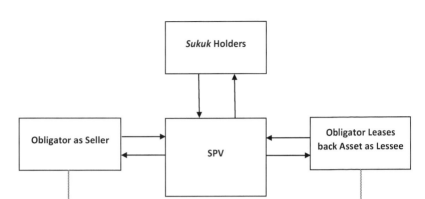

Figure 5.2 Sukuk Al-Ijarah structure

maturity of Sukuk, the special purpose entity sells back the asset to the seller at a price that is pre-determined and agreed upon between them. This price, however, should be equal to any amounts still owed under the terms of the Sukuk *Al-Ijarah*.

There are four basic methodologies to structuring leases (Mokhtar et al., 2009, p. 145):

- involving three parties with the procurement of an asset by investors from a seller and its onward lease to the obligator
- involving two parties with a sale-leaseback of the underlying property
- comprising asset securitization in which the originating party offers assets from its balance sheet into the control of depositors who enjoy the risk and return of the underliers without recourse to the initiator
- involving the lease of an asset to be delivered in the future

Sa'ad (2019) suggests that a third party that joins into the Ijarah agreement with the developers rather than the originator itself should be interested in Sukuk arrangements involving the mix of sales and lease-backed contracts. An advantage of this move would help the structure escape Inah Ijariyyah. The Sukuk structure for asset securitization cannot be exchanged on the secondary market because it includes a collateral offering that is banned under the rules of Shariah.

It is necessary to remember that Ijarah certificates or securities reflect a reasonable ownership claim over a leased asset, and, therefore, those possessing the securities have ownership liabilities that only expire until the securities mature or if they are transferred to another party who then absorbs the obligations, unlike a joint-stock company's equity shareholders (Wilson, 2004a). In addition, Ijarah certificate holders only earn from weekly, quarterly, or annual rental payments because they are unable to reap capital returns that are typically the primary incentive for stock investment. Investment in Ijarah certificates, however, is less risky than shares, and the revenue stream is for a fixed monthly amount, while any returns accruing to equity holders can differ considerably (Ahmad & Abd Rahim, 2013).

Sukuk Al-Salam

In Islamic financing terminology, the word *Salam* refers to the sale of any commodity which delivers to the purchaser at a specific time in the future, over the full payment of the current price on the spot, in advance. And, in this regard, *Sukuk Al-Salam* becomes certificates which are of equal value as that of sold commodity, issued in order to mobilize the capital so that owners of these certificates could become the owner upon the delivery of agreed commodity (Wilson, 2008). In this type of Sukuk, the party which issues the certificate is labeled as a seller of *Salam*-based goods; the party which subscribes to these certificates is termed as buyers of *Salam*-based goods; with funds realized from subscription being termed as the purchase price of *Salam*-based goods (Wilson, 2004b). Furthermore, in this type of agreement, Shariah guides both parties to not no re-sold purchased goods before the actual possession at maturity, since in this case, it will be counted as selling of debts (Zakaria et al., 2012). The recommended structure of *Sukuk Al-Salam* can be illustrated as follows:

According to the above illustration, the special purpose entity comes into an agreement with the obligator to source commodities along with buyers. Then, the obligator authorizes a contract of buying and selling with profit, the commodity, on behalf of Sukuk *Al-Salam* holders. With this on hand, *Salam* certificates are issued to investors (i.e. Sukuk *Al-Salam* holders), which are proceeded by the special purpose entity and passed to the obligator who is to sell the commodity on a further basis (Beik & Hafidhuddin, 2008). At this stage, the special purpose entity receives the commodities from the obligator, which are sold by the obligator on behalf of Sukuk holders on an agreed profit. Finally, the commodity sale proceeds are received by the Sukuk *Al-Salam* holders.

As they yield a fixed return, Salam Sukuk is a short-term (maybe 90 days) replacement for traditional bills and is deemed to be very low-risk

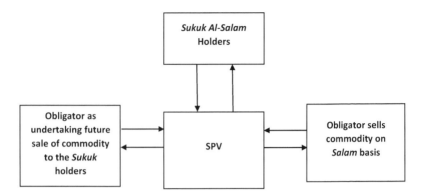

Figure 5.3 Sukuk Al-Salam structure

instruments, not least because issuers are typically sovereign governments rather than corporate customers (Wilson, 2004a). Salam Sukuk has extensive application in the agriculture sector also. Successful application of this kind of Sukuk has been witnessed in the agriculture sector of Malaysia and Indonesia (Beik & Hafidhuddin, 2008).

Sukuk Al-Murabaha

As discussed in the earlier chapters, *Murabaha* refers to the sale of goods at a particular price which includes purchase price along with an agreed and pre-defined profit. In this regard, *Sukuk Al-Murabaha* can be termed as equal value certificates issued for financing the purchase process of any particular good or commodity through the procedure of *Murabaha* and through which the holder of *Sukuk Al-Murabaha* eventually becomes the owner of a particular commodity. In similarity to the previously discussed structures of Sukuk structures, issuers of *Sukuk Al-Murabaha* become sellers of commodity, holders of *Sukuk Al-Murabaha* act as buyers of a commodity, while the funds involved in the issuance of these certificates can be taken as the timely purchasing cost of the securitized commodity (Oladunjoye, 2014). In contrast to *Sukuk Al-Salam* and *Sukuk Al-Ijarah*, there are some limitations associated with *Sukuks Al-Murabaha*. For instance, these *Sukuks* could only be negotiated in a condition that requires them to be the minor part of the package, whose constitution is dominated by procedures like *Musharakah* or Ijarah. In other conditions, the negotiations over these Sukuk items are not permitted according to Shariah perspective, since these represent debts owed from a commodity buyer to the certificate holders. In a more precise manner, such trading would result in the inclusion of Riba into the procedure.

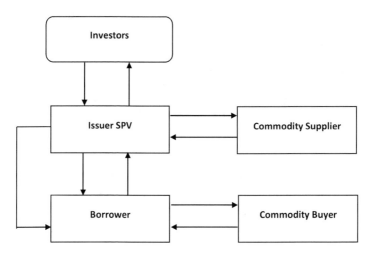

Figure 5.4 Sukuk Al-Murabaha structure

The recommended structure of Sukuk *Al-Murabaha* can be outlined as follows:

From the above illustrative representation, it can be easily extracted that it is unique from the previous two structures of Sukuk. In Sukuk *Al-Murabaha*, an agreement is first signed between the special purpose entity and the borrower and issues certificates (i.e. *Sukuks*) to the investors and buys agreed commodities from the supplier. Furthermore, this commodity is forwarded (or sold) on an on-spot basis to the borrower with a profit – an amount that is to be paid on an installment basis over a particular and pre-agreed period of time. Finally, the borrower sells the agreed commodity to the ultimate buyer and thus receives the ultimate sale price along with ultimate profit, on an on-spot basis (Muhammad & Hasan, 2020).

This Sukuk may not have a secondary market since the certificates reflect a liability owed to the certificate owned by the future seller of the asset and such trade leads to deferred debt trading for an unfair sum and this discrepancy is Riba (Godlewski et al., 2016; Shaikh & Saeed, 2010).

Sukuk Al-Musharakah

Kotilaine (2009) defines the *Sukuk Al-Musharakah* as:

> An agreement under which an Islamic bank provides funds which are mingled with the funds of an enterprise and maybe others. All providers of capital are entitled to participate in the management but are not

necessarily obliged to do so. The profit is distributed among the partners in a pre-determined manner, but the losses, if any, are borne by the partners in proportion to their capital contribution. It is not permitted to stipulate otherwise.

Regarding the discussion associated with *Musharakah*, it is a mutual relationship based on a joint venture between two parties, based on the principle of mutual loss and profit-sharing. In this regard, *Sukuk Al-Musharakah* can be termed as a document issued for utilizing the collective funds of different parties in order to engage financing into any Shariah-oriented business activity. In this type of agreement, the holders of *Sukuk Al-Musharakah* become the owners of financed business activity, with their level or percentage of ownership defined by their level of financial inclusion or fund providence. These certificates are independent and can be bought or sold in the capital markets (Saripudin et al., 2012).

The recommended structure for *Sukuk Al-Musharakah* can be illustrated as follows:

From the above-illustrated structure, it can be identified that in *Sukuk Al-Musharakah*, a corporate firm agrees with the special purpose entity to form an agreement based on the principle of *Musharakah* that is mutual profit–loss sharing in a joint venture. In this type of agreement, the corporate entity is supposed to be managing the operational activities along with the providence of fixed assets, while special purpose entity finances in this framework, which it has received from different investors (i.e. Sukuk holders)

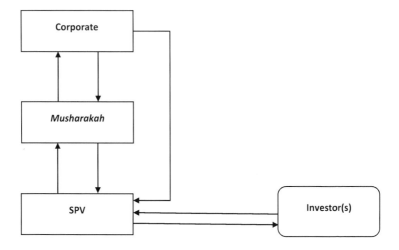

Figure 5.5 Sukuk Al-Musharakah structure

(Zakaria et al., 2012). In this manner, the corporate entity goes for leasing out the developed venture assets and gets its fixed payments along with variable incentives from the financers. Finally, the profit generated from this scheme is distributed within Sukuk *Al-Musharakah* holders, and the corporate entity goes into an agreement to buy the shares associated with special purpose entity, after a pre-agreed period of time. In other words, after the distribution of profits between Sukuk *Al-Musharakah* holders, the special purpose entity is left with no shares in the venture, as are bought by the corporate entity on the basis of as-it-is (Wilson, 2004b).

Abdel-Khaleq and Crosby (2009) pointed out a violation of Shariah rule in these types of Sukuk. It was that the originator of Musharakah Sukuk usually provides the issuer with a purchase undertaking to repurchase the underlying assets from the issuer at face value on or in the event of default on the expiry date of the Sukuk. In this case, in particular, the purchaser undertaking should not be based on the strike price but on the company dealing period or the prevailing market price on the negotiated price.

Sukuk Al-Mudarabah

The term Mudarabah can be referred to as the concept of joint-venture between two parties, over an agreement that one party should be providing the finances while the other should be involved in its careful investment into any legitimate business activity. In this type of deal, the financed party (or *Mudarib*) is bound to share the profits obtained with the financing party, on a pre-agreed ratio basis. With this concept in hand, the *Sukuk Al-Mudarabah* can be defined as security certificates issued by the *Mudarib*, in order to mobilize the funds collected from different financers, more efficiently. In such an exchange, the holder of *Sukuk Al-Mudarabah* can be termed as the financing party (according to the ratio of contribution) and the profits generated from this selling process are shared between the parties. In their constitution, *Sukuk Al-Mudarabah* is more like Shariah-oriented shares in which owners do not expect annual interests (Dusuki, 2009). Moreover, secondary trade of such a certificate is also allowed, which means, both parties can earn extra profits or losses, depending upon the value of their certificate and the activity backing it.

Jurists generally agreed that, concerning the capital that comes to his hand, the Mudarib is a trustee under a Mudharabah structure. Ultimately, the mudarib's job is to use its best efforts to make a profit for the Sukuk (i.e. rabumal) holders for whom the investment agent is entitled to pay an agreed proportion of the profit. The task of the mudarib is not to guarantee the repayment of the capital of the Sukuk in the form of a purchasing undertaking or otherwise. Similarly, unless at fault or negligence, the Mudarib cannot bear any damages from the company (Lahsasna & Lin, 2012).

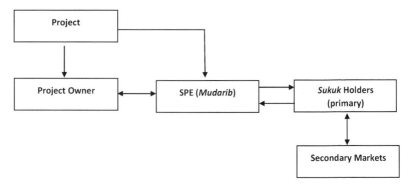

Figure 5.6 Sukuk Al-Mudarabah structure

Both partners have to determine the profit and loss ratio in the agreement to ensure transparency. The partners will, therefore, be aware that the outcomes of the partnership will be shared. The contract also often stipulates a specific percentage of the profit share of the mudharib, which is paid periodically to the Sukuk holder, in order to withdraw their investment in phases (El-Gamal, 2006; Hassan & Lewis, 2007).

In the recommended structure, it is highlighted that *Mudarib* (acting as a special purpose entity) forms an agreement with the project (business) owner for managing it and providing other fixed facilities. In this manner, it is the special purpose entity that issues Sukuk *Al-Mudarabah* and collects profits and other financial advancements that occur during the progression of the project. In the end, *Mudarib* hands over the project to its owner and thus is left with no shares in the pre-agreed project (Wilson, 2004b).

Sukuk Al-Istisna

The term *Istisna* can be defined as an agreement of production and providence of goods commodities to a party, which has paid for these goods or commodities in advance, or at a previous period of time. In this regard, Sukuk *Al-Istisna* is simply the financial security certificates, which are of equal value and are aimed at mobilizing the funds which are required for completing the production of products, which are already bought by Sukuk holders (Zakaria et al., 2012). In this type of agreement, the issuer of the certificate becomes the manufacturer of a particular commodity or product, subscribers of security certificates are genuine buyers of these products,

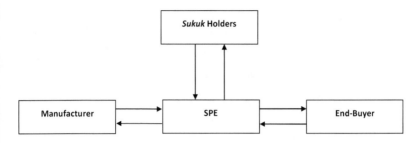

Figure 5.7 Sukuk Al-Istisna structure

while funds obtained from the mobilization process are utilized solely in the production process of agreed commodities or products (Ahmed et al., 2018).

The recommended structure of Sukuk *Al-Istisna* is very simple, outlined as follows:

In the above-illustrated structure, it can be seen that a special purpose entity is involved in the issuance of *Sukuks* and thus acting as a bridge between manufacturers of commodity or product, holders of Sukuk *Al-Istisna,* and the ultimate buyers of the product or commodity. In this structure, funds obtained from selling out of *Sukuks* are used to manufacture products and sold to the ultimate buyers. In this manner, the profits obtained from end-buyers are distributed between the Sukuk holders (Wilson, 2004b).

Conclusion

Most of the above-discussed arrangements are not strictly investment options in the raw form, but these transactions are arranged in a manner that can provide an option for the investors to earn from their capital. Like the Ijarah structure, it is basically a lease contract that is molded into an investment contract. The same is the case in Salam and Istisna. It reflects the comprehensiveness and the vastness of economic activities permissible in Islam. In a conventional system, the basic structure is single and simple which is to earn through interest on a loan, where Islam offers a lot of possible structures which can produce earning in different scenarios. Moreover, it is important to apply the arrangement in its full spirit with all its prerequisites, not merging any two of these contracts contradicting each other. This is the responsibility on the shoulders of Sharia scholars to ensure the correct application of the above-discussed structures.

References

Abdel-Khaleq, A. H., & Crosby, T. (2009). Musharakah sukuk: Structure, legal framework, and opportunities. *Sukuk, 206.*

Ahmad, N., & Abd Rahim, S. (2013). Sukuk ijarah vs. sukuk musyarakah: Investigating post-crisis stock market reactions. *International Journal of Humanities and Management Sciences (IJHMS), 1*(1), 87–91.

Ahmed, E. R., Islam, M. A., & Alabdullah, T. T. Y. (2018). The moderating role of shariah supervisory board on sukuk pricing benchmark. *International Journal of Excellence in Islamic Banking and Finance, 6*(2).

Beik, I. S., & Hafidhuddin, D. (2008). Enhancing the role of sukuk on agriculture sector financing in Indonesia: Proposed models. *Islamic Capital Markets, 85.*

Dusuki, A. W. (2009). *Challenges of realizing Maqasid Al-shari'ah (objectives of Shari'ah) in the Islamic capital market: Special focus on equity-based sukuk structures.* International Shari'ah Research Academy for Islamic Finance (ISRA).

El-Gamal, M. A. (2006). *Islamic finance: Law, economics, and practice.* Cambridge University Press.

Godlewski, C. J., Turk-Ariss, R., & Weill, L. (2016). Do the type of sukuk and choice of shari'a scholar matter? *Journal of Economic Behavior & Organization, 132,* 63–76.

Hassan, K., & Lewis, M. K. (2007). Islamic critique of conventional financing. In *Handbook of Islamic banking* (Vol. 38, pp. 38–48). Edward Elgar. https://doi.org/10.4337/9781847205414.00011

Kotilaine, J. T. (2009, March). *GCC debt capital markets an emerging opportunity.* NCB Capital Economic Research.

Lahsasna, A., Hassan, K. M., & Ahmad, R. (2018a). *Forward lease sukuk in Islamic capital markets.* Springer.

Lahsasna, A., Hassan, M. K., & Ahmad, R. (2018b). Ijarah sukuk and forward lease sukuk – case study. In *Forward lease sukuk in Islamic capital markets* (pp. 187–205). Springer.

Lahsasna, A., & Lin, L. S. (2012). Issues in Islamic capital markets: Islamic bond/sukuk. *3rd International Conference on Business and Economic Research (3rd ICBER 2012) Proceeding,* 495–512.

Mokhtar, S., Rahman, S., Kamal, H., & Thomas, A. S. (2009). *Sukuk and the capital markets.* Sweet & Maxwell.

Muhammad, M. A., & Hasan, A. B. (2020). Mudharaba and Murabaha mixed sukuk: A Fiqhi structural analysis (صكوك المضاربة والمرابحة المختلطة: دراسة فقهية تحليلية). *Journal of Islam in Asia (E-ISSN 2289–8077), 17*(2), 21–38.

Oladunjoye, M. O. (2014). Sukuk as a tool for infrastructural development in Nigeria. *Journal of Islamic Banking and Finance, 2*(1), 335–344.

Rohmatunnisa, D. (2008). *Design of Ijarah sukuk* [Unpublished MA in Finance and Investment, University of Nottingham].

Sa'ad, A. A. (2019). Structural development of ijarah sukuk: An appraisal. *Journal of Islamic Finance, 8,* 107–116.

Saripudin, K. N., Mohamad, S., Razif, N. F. M., Abdullah, L. H., & Rahman, N. N. A. (2012). Case study on sukuk musharakah issued in Malaysia. *Middle-East Journal of Scientific Research, 12*(2), 168–175.

Shaikh, S., & Saeed, S. (2010). *Sukuk bond: The global Islamic financial instrument.* Academic Press.

Wilson, R. (2004a). Overview of the sukuk market. In *Islamic bonds: Your guide to issuing, structuring and investing in sukuk* (pp. 6–7). Euromoney Books.

Wilson, R. (2004b). Overview of the sukuk market professor. In *Islamic bonds: Your guide to issuing, structuring and investing in sukuk* (pp. 3–17). Euromoney Institutional Investor Plc.

Wilson, R. (2008). Innovation in the structuring of Islamic sukuk securities. *Humanomics, 24.*

Zakaria, N. B., Isa, M. A. M., & Abidin, R. A. Z. (2012). The construct of sukuk, rating and default risk. *Procedia-Social and Behavioral Sciences, 65,* 662–667.

6 Sukuk Development in Pakistan

Muhammad AsadUllah, Rabia Sabri, Imam Uddin, Muhammad Omer Rafique, and M. Ishaq Bhatti

Introduction

This chapter is focused on the story of Sukuk in Pakistan. Pakistan has a prominent share in the global Islamic finance industry and since the inception of Islamic finance, Pakistan has been a leader in introducing new ideas, ensuring Shariah compliance and Shariah governance, and providing a human resource to the Global industry. Although the percentage share of global Islamic finance in terms of assets and issuance of Sukuk is not among the top three hubs of Islamic finance.

In this chapter, we will glance at the history of Islamic finance in Pakistan to have a clear picture of Riba-free economy movements in Pakistan. The present facts and figures will also be presented. Then we will move to the Sukuk development and issuance throughout the IF history and will discuss the hurdles that have not allowed Sukuk to flourish in the Islamic Republic of Pakistan. The chapter will end with presenting a bright future and highlighting the potential in Sukuk for the growth of this developing country.

Islamic Financing in Pakistan

Overview

Pakistan is a South Asian country with a large majority of the population as Muslims. Its official religion is Islam and its norms and cultures are deeply integrated with the teachings and events of the religion. For this reason, the Constitution of Pakistan declares Islam as its state religion (Husain, 2009) and bounds its legal system to develop any procedure or legal relationship with any law against or in objection to Islamic ideology and teachings (Constitution of Pakistan, 2010). In this regard, a resolution for the adaption of a complete legal system in accord with Islamic teachings is a thing demanded and pressed since the formation of the country in the year

DOI: 10.4324/9781003243755-6

1947. However, due to the presence of multiple sects and religions in many social and economic positions of the country, such a step is still hesitated by every government (Ahmar, 2007). In this regard, financial setup and systems based on Islamic teachings remained a great attraction for the majority of Pakistan's population, and many formal steps have been taken in the past to shift the focus of the country's capital markets from conventional financing and profit models to the model of Islamic financing. It happened in the early 1970s that major political and religious figures started voicing for a financial system free of Riba and following it, serious implementations were made in the next decade of the 1980s (Rammal & Parker, 2013).

Council of Islamic Ideology (CII) was constituted in the late 1970s as an advisory to the legislator to form Shariah-based rulings for the Islamic Republic of Pakistan. The council was given the task of homework for the reform of the economy to be Riba free. The report for CII was produced in June 1980. It offered a comprehensive mechanism for the reorganization of banking practices and procedures on the basis of mudaraba (finance trusteeship) and Musharakah (financial trust) benefit and loss sharing instruments (equity partnership). The CII study stressed that profit and loss sharing tools and qard-e-hasana would be the perfect Islamic strategies to replace interest in the banking and financial sectors (loans given to the destitute in the name of Allah) (Council of Islamic Ideology, 1980). However, inadequate measures and generalizations along with the disturbing socio-political situation of the country resisted any major shift in the financial system of markets in the country.

Finally, it happened in the year 2001 that recommendations regarding the Islamic financing system were passed by the regulatory authorities and the first Islamic bank in Pakistan started its operations. Furthermore, through these recommendations, many local banks started their Islamic banking subsidiaries – a step that remained extremely successful.

Islamic Banking Department

The Islamic Banking Department was founded by the State Bank of Pakistan in 2003. The mission of promoting and improving Shariah responsible and compliant Islamic banking as a parallel and compatible banking mechanism in the country was assigned to the department (Qureshi, 2007).

A number of Islamic financial products that can be offered by Islamic financial institutions in Pakistan have been authorized by the Islamic Banking Department. The approval of new innovative products is now regulated by the division, where every financial institution preparing to launch new Islamic financial products requires the permission of the Islamic Banking Department. The department also defines the minimum level of education and expertise that will enable a Shariah advisor to apply for practice. Banks are expected to notify the State Bank of the Shariah advisor(s) they have appointed and the related department information (Rammal & Parker, 2013).

According to a report postulated by the State Bank of Pakistan, the Islamic financing recommendation for Pakistan was based mainly on three major points:

1   Installing independent financial institutions of Islamic financing in the capital market.
2   Setting up guidelines for conventional and existing banks to start operating Islamic banking subsidiaries.
3   Allowing existing conventional banking institutions to open stand-alone Islamic banking branches.

This three-point model worked well for the country, and multiple existing banks started their Islamic banking operations, and many new entrants in the capital market started their businesses as Islamic financing and banking institutions (Islamic Banking Department, 2008).

Operations

According to the above-referenced report, the Islamic financing industry is following a unique model for its operations. This is for the reason that Pakistan is one of those Islamic countries which have remained deeply integrated with the Western conventional model of banking and finance, and large-scale implementation of any new model surely requires some approach that would seem equivalently attractive to the masses. For this reason, the State Bank of Pakistan developed a Regulatory and Supervisory Framework, in accord with the rules and laws of Shariah as well as measures of international banking sectors (Rammal & Parker, 2013). This Regulatory and Supervisory Framework suggested the position of an independent Shariah advisory board in every Islamic financing institution, in order to control, monitor, and regulate the internal and external operations of the institutions. This board is an integral part of every bank and devises its operational framework and ensures that Riba and other non-Islamic financial elements are excluded from the general and consumer banking operations (Hussain, 2008).

Furthermore, the State Bank of Pakistan also takes guidance from a dedicated Shariah compliance inspection committee and a centralized Shariah board at the State's central location. These boards and committees contain scholars and economists from different Islamic communities, who actively monitor micro and macro financing activities of the Islamic banks and thus

Table 6.1 List of Full-Fledged Islamic Banks of Pakistan that are Using Sukuk

S. No.	Name of Bank	Year of Inception	No. of Branches
1	Bank Islami Pakistan	2006	227
2	Meezan Bank	2002	799
3	Al-Baraka Islamic Bank	2004	183
4	Dubai Islamic Bank	2006	210
5	Dawood Islamic Bank	2007	–
6	Emirates Global Islamic Bank	2007	–
7	MCB Islamic Bank	2015	180

Source: (State Bank of Pakistan, 2020)

regulate the entire Islamic capital market procedures. Also, the regulatory bank and its authorities have maintained close associations with different Arabic and Middle Eastern Islamic financial institutions and Shariah advisors, to facilitate the banking process within and outside the country (Siddiqi, 2004).

Current Facts and Figures

As of the year 2020, six independent Islamic banks are operating in the country, named Meezan Bank, Al-Baraka Islamic Bank, Dubai Islamic Bank, Bank Islami Pakistan, Dawood Islamic Bank, and Emirates Global Islamic Bank.

Furthermore, conventional banking institutions of Pakistan such as Bank Al-Habib, United Bank Limited, Muslim Commercial Bank, Allied Bank, and eight other conventional banks are operating their Islamic banking chapters in a regulated and controlled environment. Moreover, financial ratings suggest that the long-awaited experiment of Islamic banking in Pakistan has proved to be extremely successful, since according to figures collected by State Bank of Pakistan the total assets of Islamic banking industry in Pakistan have amounted up to Rs 3633 billion, with a market share of money deposits as 16% of the total existing banking sector deposits (State Bank of Pakistan, 2020).

Sukuk Development in Pakistan

History

In Pakistan, Sukuk was first issued in 2005, when a foreign sovereign Sukuk of 600 million was issued by Pakistan. This Sukuk provided an semi-annual

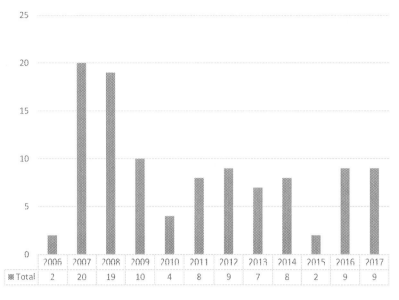

Figure 6.1 Number of Sukuk issued in the IF history of Pakistan
Source: (Ghafoor et al., 2018)

floating rate of return and was based on the agreement of Master Iajra. It was, however, first released on the Pakistani domestic Sukuk market in 2006. Since then, Pakistan has released a $695 billion Sukuk. The Sukuk market has helped Pakistan's IBs diversify their asset allocation. In addition to improving Islamic Banks' profits and performance, it presented them with an enticing investment instrument (Tareq, *et. al*. 2014).

Figure 6.1 shows that a large number of Sukuk were issued in the initial years of the Sukuk history in Pakistan that is 2007 and 2008. But the upcoming figure illustrates that these 19 Sukuk were not of large value as compared to the last five years that is since 2016. About 323 billion rupees Sukuk were issued in 2016, which is more than the sum of Sukuk issued before this year.

The State Bank of Pakistan continued to help the increasingly increasing Islamic banking sector and strengthen the system of Shariah governance that was released in 2014 and came into operation in 2015 to establish a Shariah-compliant atmosphere for Islamic financial institutions. For 2017, Pakistan worked with its market to improve its Shariah governance system in new ways, especially in the field of Fatwa statements (Laldin, 2018).

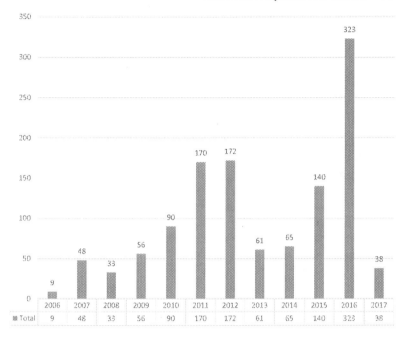

Figure 6.2 Amount of Sukuk issued in Pakistan
Source: (Ghafoor et al., 2018)

Current Situation and Recent Developments

The recent Islamic Banking bulletin of the State Bank of Pakistan reveals encouraging facts, despite the ongoing COVID-19 pandemic disturbance. It states that At the end of September 2020, IBI's (net) assets increased dramatically to 19% (Rs 170.9 billion) and stood at Rs 1070.1 billion, relative to a deceleration of 1.9% in the same duration of 2019. This rise was mainly attributed to investments made by IBIs in GOP Sukuk; GOP issued Rs 162 billion to Sovereign Sukuk during the time under scrutiny (State Bank of Pakistan, 2020).

The domestic Sukuk structure is largely based on the Islamic finance modes of Musharakah and Ijarah. As of 2017, with 75.9% volume, the Sukuk *Al-Ijarah* had the dominant share in the domestic Sukuk market as all sovereign Sukuk are focused on the Islamic Finance Ijarah model (Ghafoor et al., 2018).

The Rs 200 billion issue of Pakistan Energy Sukuk-I (PES-I) was listed on the Pakistan Stock Exchange (PSX) on 24 October 2019 (SECP, 2019).

Table 6.2 Domestic Structure of Pakistani Sukuk

Listing Status	Number of Issues	Amount in Billion Rs
Privately Placed	99	1156.58
Listed	8	47.70
Total	107	1204.28

Source: (Ghafoor et al., 2018)

PES-I is the biggest financial instrument compliant with Shariah ever listed in Pakistan on the stock exchange. The value of each Sukuk unit was placed at Rs 5,000. The minimum bid size would be 20 units or Rs 100,000. In order to address the problems facing the Islamic Pension Funds in terms of liquidity management, the decision was made due to the lack of suitable investment options open to Sharia-compliant pension funds (Ali, 2020).

Pakistan is increasingly realizing that demand and supply are guided by all market forces by the steady change toward Sukuk, rather than traditional bonds. Sukuk's major buyers are commercial banks, pension funds, workers' funds, and other financial institutions. While Sukuk has been provided for its funding needs by corporate entities such as Byco Oil Pakistan, Ghani Gases, and Fatima Fertilizer, as well as Pakistani Islamic banks such as Dubai Islamic Bank and Al Baraka Bank. In addition, the Government of Pakistan is preparing to sell USD 1 billion in Sukuk foreign currency.

Bibi and Mazhar (2019) conducted a beneficial study on six full-fledged Islamic banks of Pakistan and investigated the relationship between Sukuk and the success of the IBs of Pakistan during the last ten years from 2008 to 2017. The findings indicate that Sukuk issuance has a strong positive association between Sukuk and liquidity, although there is a significant but unfavorable connection between Sukuk and Pakistan's Islamic Banks (IB) profitability. Sukuk is an increasingly critical source of funding for banks.

Opportunities for *Sukuk* in Pakistan's Capital Markets

Pakistan is the world's second-largest Muslim nation, which has established its Islamic financing industry by the initial years of the 21st century. A large majority of its Islamic financing industry is backed up by investors and financiers from different Gulf countries, who share long-term relationships with corporate heads of Pakistan's corporate market. Furthermore, the condition of the overall Islamic financing industry within Pakistan is very strong and significant; there are six functional Islamic banks, with a Shariah regulation authority stationed at the State Bank of Pakistan, monitoring and regulating the industry process to remain in accord with Islamic corporate principles (Rammal &

Parker, 2013). Moreover, the overall financial standing of the Islamic financing industry of Pakistan is discussed in the previous sections of this study; therefore, we would specifically focus on the opportunities for *Sukuk* in this profoundly existing industry, which have not been exploited as yet.

According to Qayum and Anwar (2010), Pakistan has a strong potential for *Sukuk* and their markets. These scholars establish this assertion by realizing the efforts of Gulf-based investors to put foundations of the Sukuk exchanging markets within Pakistan's Islamic financing hubs. In its reply, the Government of Pakistan has shown keen interests in performing this experiment and selling their Sukuk bills to Gulf-based investors, with a maturity of year or less. According to Qayum and Anwar (2010), the part of state policy to double up the penetration of the Islamic financing industry into its 63-years-old corporate sector and motivate them to earn equivalent Shariah-compliant profits instead of Riba. The country's government has remained in selling its Sukuk bills in the international market, which earned USD 600 million for the country, back in 2006. It is now that the State Bank of Pakistan is looking to engage the internally existing corporate giants to involve in this activity, in order to promote the Shariah-compliant system.

Therefore, experts and economists suggest that Pakistan has quite a potential for *Sukuk* in its both corporate and retail sectors. However, this development can be taken as futuristic in its nature, since most of the financing markets that *Sukuk* will be targeting are already captured by the long-existing conventional bonds and their issuers. For this reason, it is estimated that full potential for *Sukuk* in Pakistan can only be obtained if the conventional bond market is somehow ruled out by attractive Sukuk offering, with the likes of the Malaysian system to be implemented within the country in near future.

Barriers to Sukuk Development in Pakistan

The Sukuk market in Pakistan is subjected to some specific difficulties which need to be resolved before the Sukuk market of a developed country like Malaysia can be replicated. The existence of an active secondary trading sector, for example, plays a crucial role in the Malaysian Sukuk market's success. Pakistan must also allow Sukuk to be provided with varying maturities, credit attributes, currencies, and risk profiles. As a consequence, buyers in the Sukuk market will have different options. The new Sukuk scheme in Malaysia, for instance, permits both ringgit and non-ringgit Sukuk to be released (Ghafoor et al., 2018).

Ahmad (2016) deliberated that a different and advanced regulatory system, as requested by Sukuk, is absent in many Asian countries and that this mechanism is handled under the same laws as traditional capital markets and their instruments. One of the hurdles faced by the regulators in issuing and expanding the Sukuk in the capital market is the unstructured and undocumented economy, the majority of small and medium enterprises of Pakistan do not have a documented accounts. There is a lot to be done in this regard (Dar et al., 2017).

Moreover, as history suggests that although the constitution and the appellate benches have been always pushing the government to Islamize is the whole economy and eliminate Riba, but the interest of regulatory and legislator bodies in the topic has been found discouraging in many parts of the history. That is why the stakeholders which are Shariah scholars, economists, regulators, etc. have not been able to unite to produce a real Islamic economy.

Conclusion

It is evident from the previous pages that Islamic finance has a very rich history in Pakistan which has proven that a gradual transformation is an answer to a lot of questions. As far as the Sukuk is concerned, Pakistan is progressing gradually toward the issuance of bulk quantities of Sukuk. Small investors are still not allowed to find opportunities in Sukuk. It can be a great opportunity to rule out the conventional bonds from the economic structure of Pakistan, especially with the strong religious mindsets that are existing in society.

References

Ahmad, A. U. F. (2016). Regulation, performance and future challenges of sukuk: The evidence from Asian markets. In *Advances in Islamic finance, marketing, and management*. Emerald Group Publishing Limited.

Ahmar, M. (2007). Sectarian conflicts in Pakistan. *Pakistan Vision, 9*(1), 1–19.

Ali, K. (2020, April 18). First Rs200bn sukuk issue launched via stock market. *Dawn*, p. 1. https://www.dawn.com/news/1550171

Bibi, S., & Mazhar, F. (2019). An investigation of the relationship between sukuk and the performance of banks of Pakistan. *Ijtihad: Jurnal Wacana Hukum Islam Dan Kemanusiaan, 19*(1), 53–66.

Constitution of Pakistan. (2010). *The constitution of the Islamic Republic of Pakistan*. Constitution of Pakistan.

Council of Islamic Ideology. (1980). *Report on the elimination of interest from the economy*. Council of Islamic Ideology.

Dar, M. S., Ahmed, S., & Raziq, A. (2017). Small and medium-size enterprises in Pakistan: Definition and critical issues. *Pakistan Business Review, 19*(1), 46–70.

Ghafoor, S., Saba, I., & Kouser, R. (2018). Sukuk issuance in Malaysia: Lessons for Pakistan. *Journal of Accounting and Finance in Emerging Economies, 4*(2), 159–176.

Husain, I. (2009). The role of politics in Pakistan's economy. *Journal of International Affairs*, *63*(1), 1–18.

Hussain, I. (2008). *Evolution of Islamic banking*. State Bank of Pakistan Publications.

Islamic Banking Department. (2008). *Pakistan's Islamic banking sector review 2003 to 2007*. Islamic Banking Department.

Laldin, M. A. (2018). *The shariah governance system*. https://ceif.iba.edu.pk/pdf/IFNAnnualGuide2018.pdf

Qayum, K., & Anwar, H. (2010). Pakistan plans sukuk bills to Lure Gulf banks. *Islamic Finance*. https://www.bloomberg.com/news/articles/2010-07-02/pakistan-plans-sukuk-bill-expansion-to-attract-gulf-banks-islamic-finance

Qureshi, S. (2007). The bank's new clothes. *Newsline of Pakistan*.

Rammal, H. G., & Parker, L. D. (2013). Islamic banking in Pakistan: A history of emergent accountability and regulation. *Accounting History*, *18*(1), 5–29.

SECP. (2019). *PSX lists largest ever sukuk issue*. https://www.secp.gov.pk/media-center/press-releases/psx-lists-largest-ever-sukuk-issue/

Siddiqi, N. (2004). *Islamic finance: Current legal and regulatory issues*. Social Dynamics of the Debate on Default in Payment and Sale of Debt, Presented at the Sixth Harvard University Forum on Islamic Finance.

State Bank of Pakistan. (2020). *Islamic banking bulletin*. https://www.sbp.org.pk/ibd/bulletin/2020/Jun.pdf

Tareq, M. et al. (2014). *Sukuk report*. Islamic Economic Studies.

7   Growing Opportunities in the Sukuk Markets

Muhammad Omer Rafique, Imam Uddin, Rabia Sabri, Muhammad AsadUllah, and M. Ishaq Bhatti

Introduction

This is the final chapter of this study and seeks to provide some assertive forecasts regarding the future of *Sukuks* in the global financing industry and, in particular, in the corporate financial sector of Pakistan. Moreover, this chapter also discusses recent progressions that have been made with respect to the structural evolution of *Sukuks* in global Islamic financing markets, in a brief and succinct manner.

An Opportunistic Assessment for Sukuks

According to many experts and scholars in the area of finance and economics, the global penetration of Islamic financing instruments is subjected to increase with an even more rapid pace, leading toward its face-to-face competition with dominating the conventional bond market and the stock market, in a very near future. This might have some socio-political effects as well, but increasing interests from both eastern and western parts of this globe into the Islamic financing model and its strong prevalence rule out any possibility of such event. A report compiled by *Kuwait Finance House* in 2010 stated that:

> *Islamic finance is among the fastest-growing sectors in the financial industry and has evolved to become a major part of the international financial system today. The remarkable growth has been driven by ample liquidity flows, encouraging demographics as well as the active role played by some jurisdictions around the world to promote the development of Islamic financial markets in their respective countries. The shift toward Islamic finance has gradually expanded from a personal level to a much broader corporate and institutional sphere. According to the Islamic Financial Services Board, the global Islamic*

DOI: 10.4324/9781003243755-7

finance assets are set to reach USD1.6tln by 2012 from only around USD150bln in the mid-1990s.

– Kuwait Finance House Report – 2010

Therefore, as far as the future of the Islamic financing model is considered, it is predicted and estimated as bright in nature. In this regard, discussing the opportunities currently present for *Sukuks* in global financing and specifically Islamic financing markets, we must bring into account some significant development aspects that *Sukuks* have seen in the last few years. According to Nisar (2007), *Sukuks* have enjoyed an average percentage growth rate of 144.5% in the first seven years of its introduction in Islamic capital markets. Furthermore, steps are being taken by different non-Islamic countries and their capital markets as well, to integrate *Sukuks* in their generalized format into the list of capital market instruments. Also, mentioned by Nisar (2007), most of the Islamic capital markets have employed *Sukuks* in one of the three formats listed later. These formats are also studied by conventional economists, who are willing to integrate *Sukuks* alongside conventional bonds in their respective bond markets:

Project-Based Sukuks

This is a recent development within the Sukuk market, which outlines raising and collecting money for investing into any specific project, through *Sukuks*. In the financial year 2003, successful implementation of this format was achieved by the Qatar government, which raised USD 700 million for medical health facility project, solely from Qatar Global *Sukuks*, issued on *Ijarah* basis.

Balance Sheet-Specific Sukuks

This format of Sukuk aims toward financing multiple projects of participating parties and thus achieves resource mobilization by issuing Sukuk certificates. A particular case of Islamic Development Bank (IDB) of 2003 can be mentioned in this regard, through which the bank issued more than USD 400 million *Sukuks* with a half-decade maturity period.

Asset-Based Sukuks

Under this form of development, the resources are mobilized by selling the beneficiary right of the assets to the investors (Nisar, 2007). It is the same format through which the Malaysian government started steady penetration of corporate *Sukuks* within its corporate sector and raised approximately USD 600 million in the single financial year of 2002.

Howladar (2009) stated that the term "asset-based" Sukuk simply addresses this principle in type but not in substance in most instances. The first and most critical step of any study, be it Shariah enforcement or credit risk, should be knowing the content. As per our normal credit review, we have gone through the Sukuk paperwork (sometimes hundreds of pages) in great detail in the majority of the Sukuk rated by Moody's to understand the real source of risk and source of benefit and principal/capital payments.

Actually, these developments have been made in different Islamic financing markets due to the benefits and fruitfulness offered within the structure of *Sukuks* which is discussed in detail in the later chapter of this study. As for now, we should look into some of the key benefits that *Sukuks* offer, in order to realize the growing opportunities that Islamic capital markets could offer:

1   *Sukuks* work as *Shariah*-compliant market products/financial instruments which guarantee medium or long-term fixed or variable rates of return. In this manner, a Sukuk holder in a strong capital market is assumed to attain benefits of maximum magnitudes.
2   *Sukuks* also act as liquid instruments which can be traded in secondary markets or to third parties. With this advantage, it is seen as a key element of ruling out conventional bonds from different Islamic capital markets.
3   *Sukuks* provide regulated streams of income during their investment period. Furthermore, it also offers a very easy settlement approach along with a possibility of capital appreciation.
4   *Sukuks*, through their Shariah-compliant way of operations and structure, offer a complete *Halal* source of income for investors, in accord with their Muslim faith.

With these benefits in hand, Muslim investors from different Islamic and non-Islamic capital markets see opportunities for their business to get in accord with their religion so that they can practice their religion with comfort and ease.

Global Indications

According to a formal survey conducted by Standard & Poor's in 2010, it has been reported that the global Sukuk market has reached a position from which it can start transforming the entire Islamic financing and funding industry according to the norms and regulations of Shariah. This assessment seems to be true in its nature since only in the first half of 2010, the global Sukuk issuance has reached a hallmark position of USD 13.7 billion, which is nearly as twice as the issuance amount reported in the previous year of 2009 (Damak, 2020). Moreover, according to analysts, *Sukuks* are becoming increasingly popular in the global financing industry due to their innovative way of operations, along with attractive return rates, which are competing for different financial investment products from conventional financing markets as investors turn away from real estate funds' suffering industry before and after the financial crisis period.

A case of Gulf-based investors can be cited in this regard, who in the recent crisis period of Dubai financial markets, turned their attentions toward increasingly prevailing Islamic Sukuk industry in their brother Muslim country, Malaysia. According to a report cited by Sukuk.*me*, a Gulf-based Sukuk reporting and data collecting firm, the devastating burst of the real estate bubble in the different Gulf States (including Dubai) required their respective governments and other financial authorities to cover billions of dollars in debt maturing regard. For instance, Dubai alone was/is required to cover an estimated USD 30 billion in debt maturing over a short period of two years. For this reason, investors and government authorities started eyeing the Malaysian Sukuk industry, which through intense regulation and Shariah compliance, had USD 79 billion in excess liquidity, back in the financial year 2010. This is the reason for ultimate Shariah compliancy, which was monitored by the central banking institutions of Malaysia and which resulted in the creation of more regulated Shariah-oriented secondary capital markets that Gulf countries never had.

The aforementioned case points out two important facts: due to regulated Shariah-oriented capital market in Malaysia, the effects of the global financial crisis and real estate slowdown were not faced by the investors isolated within the Malaysian capital market, and strong regulation from the central bank of Malaysia developed such standards which were uniform throughout the country. Both of these things were missing inside Gulf-based capital markets, which are hybrid as well as non-uniform in their operational nature. Through this short example, it can be realized that potential and opportunities for Islamic and non-Islamic financers and agents remain bright and encouraging within the global Sukuk market (Jobst et al., 2007).

Also, some of these global indications should be taken in an entirely separate way. Through what we have studied so far into the global trends of *Sukuks*, it can be stated that it is overall a very non-vulnerable and attractive market for different conventional and Islamic financing capital market contributors. This is all because the *Sukuks* offer the presence of underlying tangible assets, which usually have the capability of not only producing a regulated stream of revenue but also allow striving entities to pledge their significant assets for Sukuk financing. Moreover, their strong backup of fixed assets is usually considered to be ruling out the possibility of any default at the issuer-end. And for these reasons, *Sukuks* are priced linearly to provide maximum benefits for its corporate and individual holders. According to Nisar (2007), its structure is appealing in its nature, thus attracting all types of investors and financiers (i.e. from both Islamic and non-Islamic capital markets) to involve in their large-scale exchange process. Some pieces of evidence of this statement and the growing opportunities for *Sukuks* can be given as the formal enlistment of *Sukuks* in Luxembourg Exchange, London Professional Securities Market, Labuan International Financial Exchange (Malaysia), Dubai International Financial Exchange, Bahrain Stock Exchange, and Tadawul of Kingdom of Saudi Arabia.

Factual Forecasts

In the recent year, the total issuance is more than $1.35trn, around 90% of which were issued in the past ten years and 55% in the past five. In 2020, the market has proved resilient to the impact of COVID-19. In the first nine months of the year, issuance reached a total of $130.5bn, compared with $127.3bn for the same period in 2019 (Adil, 2020).

From multiple pieces of evidence that we have studied during the progression of this study (along with recent development and opportunities assessment in global and Pakistani financing capital markets), it is a very strong probability that *Sukuks* will rule out the old presence of conventional bonds and their discrete markets within different Islamic countries. Specifically, concerning the Pakistani market (which seems to be following the Malaysian Islamic financing model in its operations) is a very prospective place for the development of *Sukuks* at this particular moment. This is because the recent trend in the Pakistani bond market is observed to be of rapid emergence, as auctions of Pakistani investment bonds collectively raised 64.31 billion rupees as compared to the estimated target of 60 billion rupees (in the financial year of 2010), while Islamic financing industry is penetrating with a tremendous pace within its corporate market (*Pakistan's Bond Market on a Rising Trend,* Sukuk.me – 2010 Archives).

At this stage, if the standardized concept of *Sukuks* is introduced by Pakistan's central banking authority into countries' financial and investment markets, it will certainly attain massive attention. Although Pakistan's State Bank is currently only issuing one structure of Sukuk that is Sukuk *Al-Ijarah* (which raised 2.42 billion rupees upon its introduction in 2008), the country is all prepared for an introduction of a range of Sukuk structures within its financial sectors and is estimated to approach new horizons of success – as it did in other Islamic countries. However, the future of *Sukuks* in the global Islamic financing market is expected to be extremely impacting and significant. However, with growing uncertainty due to socio-political and social extremism factors within most of the Islamic countries, it is also possible the conventional Western bond markets will continue to capture this domain for few years in the future.

Howladar (2009) in Moody's Investor review stated that the future of Sukuk is based on the intentions of participants and stakeholders of the market. It is not only the system that is commanding instead it is the investors who can play a role in ruling out the conventional bonds from the market if they prefer the Shariah Complaint instrument in any case.

Ahmad (2016) deliberated that a different and advanced regulatory system, as requested by Sukuk, is absent in many Asian countries and that this mechanism is handled under the same laws as traditional capital markets and their instruments. Any of the regulations may be suitable for the Islamic capital market and Sukuk, but in order to handle Sukuk with good comprehension, most of these regulations require proper modification (Jobst et al., 2007).

Moving further, as far as internal developments are considered, *Sukuks* are now in the process of immense evolution and enhancements, in the global Islamic financing market. A recent development in this regard can be presented as the standardization of an entirely new structure of Sukuk, which is now being called composite or hybrid Sukuk. In a nutshell, this structure of Sukuk is also in accord with the recommendations of Accounting and Auditing Organization for Islamic Financial Institutions (AAOIFI) and is able to find its association with multiple formats of Islamic financing model at the same time that is it can have its underlying and backing pool of assets comprised of *Ijarah, Musharakah, Istisna,* etc. This type of Sukuk is not being given any particular generalization or regulation from any authority yet but is expected to be launched in the Islamic financing markets soon. This all reflects that the process of research and development is beginning within Islamic countries and is promising a bright future for global Islamic capital markets.

If, in essence, the main characteristics of cash flows, risk, and return of some Sukuk are the same as those of a traditional interest-bearing bond, then it might be better to make this transparent at the beginning to Sukuk scholars and investors. One of the implications of such openness may be that the Sukuk market is not rising as quickly as before, the other may be that the asset-backed market is more likely to exchange potential amounts. Instead of duplication, however, it is possible that it will bring some competitive and long-term benefit to the global financial system only by promoting and facilitating certain characteristics that make Islamic finance distinctive (Howladar, 2009).

Prospects

By replacing the T-bills, Sukuk has the ability to be used in performing monetary policy operations. However, in order to recognize the vision, the

Sovereign Sukuk sector is still negligible. For Sukuk to replace or be a suitable replacement for T-bills, liquidity is tremendously necessary. There is considerable demand from banks and wealth management firms for their treasury and fund management activities for more liquid Shariah-compliant investment mechanisms like Sukuk (Shaikhon, 2017).

Sukuk will also help to meet the existing infrastructure gap by improving infrastructure in Africa. There is ample land and natural capital in Africa. This makes Africa and other emerging areas a profitable market for the issuance of Sukuk that can be funded by real estate. In the economic systems of many African countries, agriculture remains the mainstay. Sukuk will, thus, be used to fund new technology and modernize agriculture (Shaikhon, 2017).

Recommendations for Future Studies

Sukuks have much to offer in the research process of their structures and operational characteristics for those, who are well versed with the concept of Shariah and its rulings in different corporate and state-based financial activities. In this regard, this study makes a solemn recommendation for future researchers to make literary attempts and generalizing or standardizing the concept of hybrid/composite *Sukuks*, so that, more instruments like this along with other structures would come into the market to compete with the strong conventional bond markets. Also, a prospective research path could be taken to identify the trend of different Islamic financing instruments and their acceptability in different Islamic and non-Islamic markets, in order to judge (through comparative analysis) which one has remained most successful. This type of research path would let the researcher identify with what specific products and offerings Islamic financing industry can prepare to compete with conventional financing and bond markets.

In shape, but not in material, many of the existing Sukuk forms conform to AAOIFI. It is recommended to provide a transparent credit review that can help sustain a stable and long-term Sukuk market so that investors are completely aware of the true existence of such securities. At a later point, this helps avoid creditor lawsuits should the corporation or properties become troubled (Howladar, 2009).

References

Adil, M. (2020, October 19). 2020: A strong year for sukuk. *Refinitiv*, *1*.

Ahmad, A. U. F. (2016). Regulation, performance and future challenges of Sukuk: The evidence from Asian markets. In *Advances in Islamic finance, marketing, and management*. Emerald Group Publishing Limited.

Damak, M. (2020). *Islamic finance outlook*. Islamic Finance.

Howladar, K. (2009). *The future of sukuk: Substance over form?* Moody's Investors Service.

Jobst, A., Kunzel, P., Mills, P., & Sy, A. (2007). *Islamic bond issuance – what sovereign debt managers need to know.* https://www.imf.org/external/pubs/ft/pdp/2008/pdp03.pdf

Nisar, S. (2007). *Islamic bonds (sukuk): Its introduction and application.* www.financeinislam.com

Shaikhon, S. A. (2017). *Future sukuk growth depends on overcoming challenges.* Islamic Economics Project Website. Retrieved January 16, 2020, from https://islamiceconomicsproject.com/2017/11/15/future-sukuk-growth-depends-on-overcoming-challenges/

Index

Printed in the United States
by Baker & Taylor Publisher Services